**Personal Safety Strategies
That Can Keep You
From Becoming
A Target
Of
Crime & Violence**

Joseph C. Martini, **CPSI**

First Edition

CPO Publishing
Spokane, Washington

HARD TARGET
Joseph C. Martini, CPSI

Published by:

CPO Publishing
P.O. Box 14081
Spokane, Washington 99214

All rights reserved. No part of this book may be reproduced or transmitted in any form or by any means, electronic or mechanical, including photocopying, recording or by any information storage and retrieval system without the express written approval from the author and publisher, except for brief quotations in a review, or crime prevention seminars.

Copyright © 2000 by Joseph C. Martini

Printed in the United States of America

Library of Congress Cataloging-in-Publication Data

LCCN - Library of Congress Control Number: 2002115410
HARD TARGET: Personal Safety Strategies That Can Keep You from Becoming a Target of Crime & Violence / Joseph C. Martini – 1st Ed.

Includes credits, references, and index
ISBN No. 0-9725985-0-2

Cover Graphics: J.C. Martini
Edited by: Laura Torsiello
Interior Design and Typesetting: Karen Erbe Cappiello
Printed by: Palm Springs Printing, Altamonte Springs, Florida

For Linda

"Keep up the good work!"

Joseph C. Martini
11/17/04

A Word from the Author

The ability to predict and protect oneself from crime and violence is an inbred instinct dating to the dawn of man. Men and women will always react to danger in any form. Against themselves, their family, and certainly their children, but how they react will determine the outcome. Some will adapt a passive attitude, trusting that some measure of compassion and mercy can be found in the aggressor. Others will be paralyzed in fear, and find themselves incapable of defending themselves. Some will react in anger, blindly striking out with uncontrolled and defiant reaction. Conversely, a small minority will have the skills and training to logically, calmly, and quickly, assess the situation and focus on the danger. They will automatically draw on their Crime Management training to minimize the risk, and survive. They have a plan – Do you?

Sadly, most citizens do not handle crime and violence very well. Even though we are reminded almost daily of the dangerous predators in every community in America, most think it will never happen to them, it will only happen to the other guy – but think about that for a moment, to the *other* guy – *you* are the other guy. I call that the ostrich syndrome. If you stick your head in the sand you cannot see the danger, therefore it does not exist. Take your head out of the sand. Crime and violence is not something you should fear, or hide from. With proper training, it is something you can manage and survive. If you have a plan of action *before* you find yourself in harm's way, you have a significantly better chance of controlling the outcome.

October 1994, Goldenrod, Florida:
A dramatic four-hour standoff between deputy sheriffs and an armed, distraught man, Robert Abbarno, terrified the staff, clients, and owner of a nail salon in this quiet suburb of Winter Park, Florida.

Estranged with the owner of the salon, Abbarno, stormed into the busy salon armed with a .357 caliber Magnum revolver, and quickly took everyone hostage.

Upset and enraged with anger, he threatened to kill everyone, including himself. One of the staff told him to "get out. You are under a restraining order." Without hesitation, he pointed the weapon directly at her face and pulled the trigger – the weapon misfired. He then held the deadly weapon against the temple of the owner, said he was going to kill her, himself, and anyone else that did not leave immediately.

After four harrowing and tension-filled hours, it was over. Thanks to the excellent hostage management efforts of Sheriff Don Eslinger, of the Seminole County Sheriff's Office, and members of their elite SWAT Team, the incident was resolved without injury or loss of life.

Not one person in that salon was expecting the violence and danger that suddenly burst through those doors. Some had no contingency plans to rely on, and some did. Cynthia, the salon owner, remained calm and supportive for the terrified customers and staff (she later faked a heart attack to effect her release from the abductor. The other person with presence of mind and faith, said, "Come on girls, he wants us to leave, and he won't hurt us. Let's all leave now." She calmly led the customers and staff out of harm's way. In case you missed the name in the earlier paragraph, that person was my wife, Cherie Martini. I was so proud of her. Crime prevention training paid big dividends on that frightening day in small town America.

Robert Abbarno was charged with false imprisonment, attempted murder, aggravated assault, and felony stalking. He was subsequently sentenced to 12 years in the Florida prison system. He has threatened to kill all those involved upon his release.

It does not always happen to the other person... Sometimes it hits home with chilling clarity. What would your reaction be? Do you have a plan? I would like to help. Read this book, and others like it, then pass them along to a friend or loved one. You could save a life.

Post Script:

Less than a year later, Cynthia, the owner of the salon, was married. Four months later, her new husband strangled her, then he shot and killed himself. The reason – credit card debt.

Acknowledgment

First, I would like to thank my wife, Cherie, and my lovely daughter, Jana, for their encouragement and understanding while writing this book. Their confidence and support provided the foundation necessary for a difficult project of this nature.

My appreciation also includes my extended family – Nick, Kathy, Mark, Troy Nickerson, and Kip. Nicholas and Pat Nickerson, Madge and Jimmy. A special thanks to Jose Mena. Everyone, thanks for believing in me and never doubting the value of this book.

I would be remiss if I failed to express my gratitude to everyone at Johnny's Diner in Orlando, Florida. Johnny Krasniqi (the owner and my best friend), his lovely wife, Margarita. Thanks, also, to Fred and Linda Prekaj, and Pashka Krasniqi. A special thanks to "Mom" and the other regulars and staff. Thanks for keeping my coffee cup full and my spirit nourished with positive reinforcement. There are many others, too numerous to mention. However, you know who you are, and you should know how I greatly appreciate your support.

During initial research and development of Hard Target, I quickly realized that the complexities and diversity of subject matter were beyond the scope of one person. Therefore, I would like to acknowledge the many contributors that supported this book, provided copyright use, and offered professional advice. Hard Target is a good example of crime prevention practitioners, and citizens alike, coming together for a common cause; to take a proactive approach to crime and violence.

WITH APPRECIATION:

- John F. Kennedy (Quotation)
- FBI Uniform Crime Reports
- REACT International
- Bureau of Justice Statistics
- AAA Auto Club South
- Joseph T. Chew (Quotation)
- US Department of Justice Press
- US National Crime Victimization Survey
- Associated Press
- Marilyn Ferguson (Quotation)
- National Insurance Crime Bureau
- BJS
- US Justice Department
- Seminole County, Florida Sheriff's Office
- Albert Einstein (Quotation)
- Insurance Information Institute
- WYC (National watch your car program)
- US Bureau of Justice Assistance
- FDLE – Florida Department of Law Enforcement
- C.A.T. Program
- LoJack
- Gaven De Becker, Author, "The Gift of Fear"
- National Center for Crime Victims
- National Victims Center
- National Crime Prevention Council
- National Sheriff's Association
- International Society of Crime Prevention Practitioners
- David H. Caster, ISCPP
- Elias Conetti (Quotation)
- National Youth Gang Survey
- The United States Office of Juvenile Justice
- Lisbeth Schorr, Author – "Within Our Reach"

- [ ] National Foundation For Abused and Neglected Children
- [ ] SEGAC, Southeastern Gang Activity Group
- [ ] William Gladden Foundation
- [ ] Reno, Nevada Police Department
- [ ] Robert Walker, Gangs or US (Website)
- [ ] Family Violence Prevention Fund
- [ ] Lynne Lee FVPF, Director of Public Education
- [ ] Center for Research Policy
- [ ] Kaiser Permanente Poll
- [ ] TRIAD
- [ ] Costra County Sheriff's Office
- [ ] MADD, Mothers Against Drunk Driving
- [ ] National Association of State Units on Aging
- [ ] NCMEC, National Center for Missing and Exploited Children
- [ ] Cecil Greek
- [ ] Center for Study and Prevention of Violence
- [ ] National District Attorneys Association
- [ ] Neighbors Who Care, Prison Fellowship Ministries
- [ ] C. Taylor, Researcher "Girls, Gangs, Women and Drugs"
- [ ] Sammy "The Bull" Gravano
- [ ] National Rifle Association
- [ ] Encarta
- [ ] Gary Fleck & Mark Gertz
- [ ] Journal of Criminal Law & Criminology
- [ ] National Vital Statistic Report
- [ ] Lawrence Southwick, Jr. "Guns and Justifiable Homicide"
- [ ] Archives of Internal Medicine
- [ ] FSU – Self Defense Study
- [ ] Taser International
- [ ] BJS – Criminal Victimization Changes
- [ ] Harold Torsiello

About the Author

Joe has been involved and researching law enforcement and crime prevention issues for over 30 years. He has been married to his lovely wife, Cherie, for over 27 years, and has a 23-year-old daughter, Jana, who currently resides in the Bahama Islands.

Disclaimer

This book was designed and published to help the readers establish a personal safety strategy (A plan <u>not</u> to be a victim of crime and violence). While the primary goal is awareness and avoidance, we understand that 100% safety is not possible due to the unpredictability of human behavior. With this in mind, readers are advised to view this publication as a book of options.

While we live in a society of laws, we are also surrounded by a lawless element. To be aware that these criminals do exist, and realizing we can become victims at any moment, is the first step in crime management and personal safety. The responsibility for personal protection is not the primary duty of the police. Personal protection is the responsibility of each adult citizen, and that person is responsible for the safety of his or her children, while keeping in mind that protection must always conform to the rules of law.

This book is intended to provide information about crime and violence, and help the readers develop personal safety strategies before they are victimized. This is a book about awareness, avoidance and options. The publisher, author, and contributing authors are not engaged in rendering legal advice. If legal or other expert assistance is required, the readers are advised to seek legal council, or consult with law enforcement professionals appropriate to their needs.

This book was never to be the definite answer to everyone's crime management needs, but it can supplement other publications dealing with crime and violence. Readers are urged to seek out other books on crime prevention, attend self-help crime prevention seminars, and participate in programs and activities provided by law enforcement professionals in their communities.

Every effort has been made to assure the accuracy of content, but typographical, and subject matter errors are sure to happen to the best of writers and editors. In addition, statistical data can be difficult to adjust with the constant ebb and flow of crime. Some crime statistics are only made available every four or five years. Consequently, this book should be used as a general guide intended to peel back the layers of apathy, and make the readers realize that criminals are not little trolls that live under bridges. They are very real, often dangerous, and they are constantly looking for targets of opportunities.

This publication is meant to entertain and educate. The authors and publisher accept neither liability nor responsibility to any person or entity regarding loss or damages caused or alleged to be caused, directly or indirectly, by information found in this book.

Table of Contents

Chapter One: Vehicle/Travel Security   Page 1

- Predators have plans for travelers
- Contingency planning
- Traveling alone
- Ted Bundy
- Safety tips
- Cell phones
- Bogus cops.
- Vehicle breakdowns
- REACT
- Avoid traveling alone.
- Road rage
- AAA Auto Club
- Examples, stories, and options

Chapter Two: Carjacking   Page 19

- Carjacking popularity
- Child dies from carjacking
- Escaping police pursuit
- 200,000 hijacked cars exported
- Teen Carjackers
- 80% of Carjackers are armed
- Intentional accidents, predator's plan
- Convenience stores can be dangerous
- Stop light trap
- Public parking hunting ground
- Criminal patterns and attitudes
- Resistance / pro and con
- Safety strategies that work
- Creative survival options
- All age groups are targets
- Be proactive and reduce your risks
- Profiling and surviving, and more

Chapter Three: Auto and Property Theft Page 36

- Auto theft is a growth business
- Vehicle stolen every 17 seconds
- U.S. Dept. of Justice release
- Locked door policy
- Avoidance and non-confrontation
- Crime management techniques
- Don't let him take you and the car
- Joy-ride theft…you can be charged
- Statistical data, and common sense ideas

Chapter Four: Anti-Theft Devices Page 43

- Multi-million dollar industry
- Three reasons for auto theft
- Organized crime "chop shops"
- Joy riding
- Secondary use for stolen
- Vehicle Anti-theft alarm technology
- Selecting an alarm
- Insurance considerations
- Security options that meet your needs
- Levels 1 through 4
- Alarm types and function
- Beware of code hopping
- VIN number glass etching
- Watch your car program
- C.A.T. Program
- 42 Officers feloniously slain
- Traffic control and vehicle stops
- LoJack location and recovery system
- Systems that prevent auto theft
- Suggested reading list

Chapter Five: Home Security　　　　　**Page 60**

- No house is "burglar proof"
- Building blocks for a safe community
- Starting your crime prevention plan
- Becoming proactive
- Beware of "Lock" thieves
- Is there an alligator in the lake?
- FBI Crime Reports
- Establish a locked door policy. Now!
- Preventive measures for burglary
- Doors, windows, and best options
- How to stop a burglary
- Hardening your home
- Safe rooms
- National Center for Crime Victim reports
- Neighborhood watch program

Chapter Six: Gangs　　　　　**Page 81**

- U.S. Office of Juvenile Justice & Delinquency
- Brush with danger
- Gang survey
- $450 billion cost
- Family structure
- Lisbeth Schorr
- Primary cause
- Media influences
- Girls, gangs, women, drugs
- Early warning signals
- Recommended books & videos
- Reno case history
- Gang names (Nation-wide)
- Graffiti
- Violent confrontation
- Colors

Chapter Seven: Domestic Violence **Page 98**

- Dangerous society
- Growing crime problem
- 960,000 incidents
- Breaking the silence
- FVPF
- Karen's story
- Paul's story
- Remarks by Paul
- Physical battering
- Intimidation
- Assault
- Psychological violence
- Unwanted sexual violence
- Many faces of battery
- Most common killer of women
- Date rate
- Kaiser Permanente Poll
- Breaking the cycle
- Resources

Chapter Eight: Senior Citizen Crime Prevention **Page 114**

- Awareness/Avoidance/and Safety Strategies
- Apathy makes a victim
- Psychological impact
- Senior crimes by types
- 46,000 purse snatchings
- Rape, robbery, and aggravated assaults
- Murder
- Crime demographics
- Dignity & Privacy
- Warning signals
- Personal safety planning
- 4 step plan
- Safety strategies

- Dogs
- BBB – Better Business Bureau
- Telemarketing crimes
- Triad
- AARP
- National Sheriff's Association
- Police
- Neighborhood Watch Program

Chapter Nine: Child Crime Prevention**Page 132**

- When to teach safety
- Nat. Cntr. For Missing & Exploited Children
- Options for children
- 8 rules for safety
- Adult supervision
- Children abducted
- Pre-planning
- Statistics
- Friendly stranger
- Victims by gender
- Teen communication
- "The Front Line"
- Assistance for families
- Child pornography
- Sexual exploration
- Tip-Line

Chapter Ten: Firearms**Page 138**

- Lethal force
- Option of last resort
- Home, family, and business defense
- Pro-rights / Anti-gun advocates
- Technological explosion
- Firearm safety
- "Sammy the Bull"
- Sudden Confrontation

- Psychological aftermath
- NRA
- Self-defense issues
- Second amendment
- Domestic homicide
- Self defense study
- 2nd leading cause of death
- Successful civilian firearm defenses
- Women at high risk
- Kids & Guns
- Saves a life every 1.3 minutes
- Firearms – A family decision

Chapter Eleven: Non-Lethal Self Defense   Page 144

- Dangerous environment
- Mental and physical preparation
- Face-to-face with physical danger
- Physical training
- Martial arts
- Personal alarms
- Countermeasure products
- 25.9 million victimizations
- Stun guns technology
- Air Tasers
- Pepper spray
- History of OC – Oleoresin capsicum
- Pepper spray and law enforcement
- Use of personal restraint canisters
- Dangerous aggression restraint
- Criminal triangle
- Benefits of OC
- Limitations of OC
- Habanera – World's hottest
- Non-Lethal Response

CHAPTER ONE

Vehicle/Travel Security

"Take time to repair the roof when the sun is shining."
— President John F. Kennedy

Motor vehicles and travel in general increase our chances of becoming a victim. As we travel about the cities we live in, or across the country, we travel through areas of danger without even thinking about it. Moving in the air-conditioned comfort of our locked cars, listening to our favorite music, lulls us into a false sense of security. Our focus is on our travels. Going to work, visiting friends, shopping, or simply enjoying the countryside while on a business trip, or vacation. Our only plan is the reason for the drive. The predators along the way also have plans, but they are vastly different from those of honest citizens. These people make their living by crimes of opportunity. A motorist out of gas, a flat tire on a dark and deserted roadway, a lost and disoriented driver asking a stranger for directions, or an act of good will for a hitchhiker on a cold night - all potential disasters waiting to happen. Think about the distance you can travel in a car, as opposed to foot travel. On foot we are limited to a small area, and that means a smaller number of predators. Driving allows us to cover a much greater distance and puts us in the general area of more people looking for an opportunity to rob someone. It is simply a numbers game. If you drive, eventually you will find yourself in a potentially dangerous situation. How you handle the problem will depend on your crime prevention training. If you do not have a contingency plan, you will most likely become tomorrow's news.

MAKE SAFETY YOUR LONG TERM GOAL.

EXAMPLE:
It is a bright, sunny day and a young woman is on a well-deserved vacation when she decides to exit the freeway for gas and a cold Pepsi. As she pulls into a busy convenience store, she feels comfortable because of the number of men, women and children at the store. Although she is a woman traveling alone, she feels at ease. This could well be the store in her neighborhood back home. As she enters the store, the laughter of children and the bright Spring day gives her a warm glow of peace and good will. The young woman is really starting to enjoy her vacation drive. As she begins filling her gas tank, she notices a young, well-dressed man waiting by the pump, gas can in hand. He starts a pleasant, casual conversation as she continues to pump the gas. "Take your time miss, I'm in no hurry," he says. "Dumb bunny me, I ran out of gas. I'm the youth pastor for my church and I'm always harping at the kids to drive off the top half of the tank and not the bottom half. I will never be able to live this down," he says, a wide-open, friendly grin spreading across his handsome face. "I'm only about four blocks from the church, but with my bum knee I guess I'll miss music practice…say, would it be an imposition for you to run me up to the church? I really don't want to leave the kids unsupervised for very long…you know kids. I'll introduce you to them. They'll think you're a hero for rescuing their youth pastor."

She quickly sizes him up. She had always prided herself on her ability to read people. Six feet tall, dark, wavy well-groomed hair, expensive dress slacks, stylish loafers, white shirt and tie. Coupling all that with a great smile and a winning personality made her very comfortable doing a good deed for a youth pastor. She drove out of the friendly convenience store with her new friend. What a great vacation this was turning into. Unfortunately, things are not always, as they appear. **DON'T GIVE RIDES TO CASUAL STRANGERS!** The profile of that young preacher matches the profile of **Ted Bundy.** Do I have your attention? This was a fictional account designed to illustrate a point, but Ted Bundy was horrifyingly real.

"What's one less person on the face of the earth anyway?"
— Ted Bundy
PS: Ted Bundy was executed in 1989. He allegedly killed 36 women.

I believe it is important that we establish our own personal comfort zone. By our very nature, we seek out environments that are free from the threat of aggression. We need to know that we have a secure space in which we can be safe...a foot, five feet, arm's length, or the security of our locked vehicle or home - a personal comfort zone that can only be violated by invitation. Be very careful whom you send out invitations too.

Creating a safe environment has a VALUE. When you have something of VALUE, you take care of it. When you have something of VALUE that you take care of, it can last a lifetime.

- Do not ever give rides to casual friends or strangers... **Never!**
- Do not pick up hitchhikers.
- Do not engage in idle conversation with strangers.
- *Always* carry something of a defensive nature in your car and on your person. Pepper Spray is recommended (Pepper Spray will be covered in the Non-lethal Self Defense chapter).
- Do not let anyone know you are traveling alone. Be a part of a "Convoy," or keep a dummy covered with a blanket in the back seat creating the appearance of someone asleep.
- Do not dress provocatively.
- Walk with an "in control" attitude.
- Do not discuss your destination or where you are staying for the night. Someone could overhear this conversation and take it as an opportunity to perpetrate a crime against you.
- Establish a locked door policy – lock doors as soon as you enter or exit your vehicle.

- Sound your horn if threatened by aggressive behavior.
- Install a vehicle alarm but do not use a standard auto alarm siren. Have you ever heard a car alarm siren going off? Did you pay any attention? Of course not, too many false alarms. Have your car alarm <u>interfaced</u> with your horn and lights. When you have an alarm, condition the headlights and tail lights begin flashing. The horn will start honking…everyone pays attention when a horn honks. Flashing lights and blaring horn will cause even the most seasoned thief to look for greener pastures.
- Install a hidden ignition cutoff switch. If a thief tries to steal your car, with or without the keys, it will not run with the ignition bypassed. Simple and to the point. If it will not start, it cannot leave home without you.

AUTO THEFT SECTION WILL COVER VEHICLE ALARMS AND ANTI-THEFT DEVICES IN MORE DETAIL.

- Stay away from known trouble areas. Plan your route to avoid high crime neighborhoods.
- Fill your gas tank when it is half-empty. An ounce of prevention is worth a pound of cure.
- Beware of scams like "Intentional Accidents" (deliberate minor fender benders designed to make you stop). You are then a prime target for carjacking, rape, pillage, or plunder. If involved in a simple "fender-bender," do not stop. Signal to the other party that you are going to stop, but not in some isolated and vulnerable location. Turn on your 4-way flashers, and then slowly drive to a safer, populated area.
- If you are ordered to get into a car with a bad guy, don't go there, as your chance of survival is marginal at best. They do not need you in the car to rob you, or steal your car. Give them your keys, your purse, scream, run, pass out, vomit…do whatever it takes to get away, but don't get in that car. If possible, Pepper Spray directly in the face will definitely get the point across that you are going to refuse to be a victim.

Chapter One							Vehicle/Travel Security

- Report any suspicious activity or attempted crime to the police as soon as possible. Remember that personal protection begins with personal responsibility. Do not be afraid to get involved. Press charges and help reclaim our streets.
- Keep a cell phone in your vehicle programmed for 911. Take it into your motel when you travel. Carry it on your person when shopping, and keep it in your master bedroom when you are at home. It can save your life, or help someone else in distress.

WHY DOESN'T EVERYONE CARRY A CELL PHONE?

One reason is cost. Cellular phone costs, activation fees, and monthly service charges can be expensive. I will let you in on a little secret. Did you know that once a cell phone has been activated, and then turned in or sold for whatever reason, by Federal Law, it must be able to dial 911 FREE OF CHARGE? All that is required is a charged battery and it can dial 911 any place in the United States, completely free of charges. You do not have to subscribe, or pay a monthly service fee. Go to pawnshops, flea markets, or garage sales, and buy a used one for twenty or thirty dollars and you can then reach an emergency operator if the need ever arises. You can ONLY dial 911, but all it will cost is the price of the phone. I purchased mine in a garage sale, purchased a cigarette lighter adapter from Radio Shack, and my total investment was less than thirty-five dollars. Make this a required security item when you travel, and do not go anywhere without it.

- Whenever you leave the vehicle, take the cell phone with you: Shopping, walking, jogging, your work place, and in your home. It does not matter if it is a full service cellular or simply one that dials 911 only. It can save your life, or help someone else that has an emergency. REMEMBER: Using a cellular requires that you give the operator your location and good direction for emergency personnel. Unlike a normal phone that displays the location of the caller on a computer monitor when dialing 911, cellular phones cannot be accessed by computer

❏ location software. Stay calm, take a deep breath, and give the operator your address or good landmarks and directions. Carefully and calmly, follow the instructions of the operator. I often think about the story of the boater capsizing her canoe. Alone in the middle of the lake, clinging to her inverted canoe; she was able to use the cell phone she had clipped on her waist belt to dial 911. She was very lucky the water had not damaged the phone. The startled emergency operator was able to direct rescue personnel as the woman clung to the canoe giving directions. It most definitely got her out of harm's way, and most likely saved her life. She could not swim.
❏ Cellular Telephones: A must-have security device, but do your best to keep them dry.

BOGUS COPS

QUESTION: You are driving on a dark highway or street; you look in your rear view mirror and see flashing lights, presumably a police officer. What do you do? What is your plan? Do you even have a plan? Most law abiding citizens would pull to the side of the road, stop, activate their emergency flashers, roll the window down, and wait for the officer to tell them why he was stopping them. This might not be your best option. Unless you can <u>clearly</u> identify the vehicle as a police car, and <u>clearly</u> identify the driver as a police officer, **you would be best advised not to stop on a dark and isolated roadside**…keep moving, but not before you do a few things. Acknowledge to the driver that you see him, and you are going to stop, but not before you get to a well-lit and public place. You can signal your intent by waving, turning on your hazard lights, slowing down, and turning on your interior lights, then proceed to a public place like a convenience store, gas station, or even a fire or police station. If it is a phony cop, and they are out there, what do you think he is going to do? You're right! He takes off, and you are out of harm's way. Better safe than sorry. However, if you <u>can</u> clearly identify the vehicle as a police car, pull to the side of the road and shut your engine off. If it is after dark, activate your flashers, turn your dome light on, roll your window down, keep both hands on the steering wheel, and wait for instructions from the officer. There is a very valid reason for following that protocol when being stopped by a legitimate law enforcement officer. A press release issued *May 15, 2000 by the FBI National Press Office, said that preliminary statistics indicate that nationwide there were 42 law enforcement officers feloniously slain in the line of duty in 1999, the lowest recorded figure in more than 35 years. In 1998 there were 61 officers killed in the performance of their duty to the public.

This significant reduction is due in part to stiffer sentencing guidelines, a stronger position on handguns, and increased training. But when you cut through all of the statistical babble, 42 officers killed in the line of duty certainly grabs the attention of those officers that are on the line, and today they are using more caution on the job. Simply put, especially when it comes to traffic stops, they are not inclined to be mister nice guy...they are all business. They are now going to approach a suspect with extreme caution, even for a simple traffic stop. What is the point of saying all this? Work with them. They have a very dangerous job, and they are putting themselves on the line for all of us; a thin blue line between us and the dangerous criminals. Let us try to understand their caution, present an attitude of cooperation, and do not allow a traffic stop by police officers to escalate into a more serious situation. Remember that a police officer is charged with controlling criminal violations, misdemeanors and felonies alike, as well as meeting due process constraints...Work with them and they will try to make the process as comfortable and painless as possible. This is in everyone's best interest. Relax; take your citation, and maybe you will only receive a warning ticket...stranger things have happened.

- ❏ If you suspect a bogus cop, use a cell phone and call for help.
- ❏ If an unmarked "alleged" police car follows you to a public area and you are still not convinced he is a real cop, from the security of your locked car, have him call a marked patrol unit to the scene before opening your door.

BADGE OF AUTHORITY

QUESTION: What do you do if you are driving along in daylight, and a plain unmarked car pulls along side of your vehicle with a flashing red or blue strobe light on the dash? Then the driver holds up a badge and ID Wallet and motions you to pull to the side of the road. Would you recognize this as a badge of authority and comply? Unless you see verifiable markings, or a license plate that clearly identifies this car as a police vehicle, or the driver has on a police uniform, don't stop! Blue and red lights are legal for anyone to buy in many states. The law allows you to buy these products, but makes them illegal to use illegally…go figure! The badge: I purchased a Deputy United States Marshal badge, Federal ID, and badge wallet at a specialty shop on International Drive in Orlando, Florida for thirty five dollars, no questions asked. I had a passport-sized photo taken at a photo machine at Kmart, typed the ID on my daughter's typewriter, and laminated it. The disclaimers on the receipt for the badge and ID said for use as a novelty only. The badge and identification card look **very** authentic. Anyone can buy these items in specialty shops, spy shops or costume shops in most major cities in America. If you go on the Internet you can even download authentic looking ID's that can turn you into whoever you want to be; police officer, doctor, cab driver, private eye, pilot, even an ordained minister…and the list goes on. For the really professional thief, there are thousands of illegal sources for bogus ID badges (some collectors will even sell real badges to complete strangers), police caps, uniforms, and even body armor. By the way, a bulletproof vest is legal to own in most states, and only becomes illegal if it is used in the commission of a crime. Stencil a bulletproof vest with POLICE, or FBI, wear it on the outside of a black jump suit, a cap with press on letters announcing POLICE or FBI, and you have everything you need for a home invasion. How about a master's degree in Police Sciences…piece of cake in Cyber Space. If it walks like a duck, quacks like a duck, and looks like a duck…it is not necessarily a duck! If in doubt, use your cell phone. Call a cop…a real cop! If confronted by someone out of uniform, or in a uniform you have doubts about, ask him to call a cop...a real one! Don't worry, if he's a real law enforcement officer, he will understand. He might not like it, but he will understand.

VEHICLE BREAKDOWNS

A vehicle can be a wonderful beast of burden, and for some, almost a love affair. But when they break down on us, that wonderful relationship can turn ugly in a heartbeat. It is important for everyone to realize that the highways of America can be extremely dangerous, and all too often, fatal. Keep your vehicle maintained, and do a complete maintenance service before any extensive travel. Breakdowns on the roads are a breeding ground for crime and violence. A valuable part of your travel plan should include a safety strategy in the event of a vehicle breakdown on the road. There are many reasons that cause us to pull to the side of the road, but let us just concern ourselves with three primary reasons.

- Vehicle overheats
- Run out of gas
- Flat tire

There is not much you can do about a car overheating unless you are close to a water source. That may get you off the road and to a safer location to address the problem, but most likely, you will need repairs, or a wrecker. Most common reasons for overheating include a ruptured water hose, broken water pump belt, or the water pump can go bad, causing a major leak. In cold weather, climates a freeze plug in the engine block can spring a leak. Get on the cell phone. Be quick about it. Keep your doors locked. Don't accept help from strangers. If they offer, from the locked privacy of your vehicle, ask them to stop and report your location and problem to the nearest wrecker or police officer. Flag down a passing patrol car. I have heard of people carrying a jug of water for emergencies, but most experts agree it will provide very limited relief, at best, but they admit it can't hurt anything. With a small leak it might get you to a safe area to address your problem. If space is not a problem, carry a plastic jug of water on your trip.

Running out of gas will bring a pleasant drive to a quick stop. Although you could carry the new synthetic type emergency fuel in your trunk, it is hard to find, and could be dangerous if improperly stored and handled. Seems like a plug for AAA is in order at this point. Good luck. Next time - if there is a next time, drive off the top half of your gas tank.

Flat tires are the leading cause of vehicle breakdowns on our roads. It is highly dangerous to drive on a flat tire and should only be attempted if you are in a life-threatening situation, but there is something you may want to do as a preventative measure. Carry a can of "Flat Fix" in your trunk. This is a small aerosol can of material that will inflate the tire, and if the damage is not too severe, seal the leak. You simply attach the nozzle to your valve stem and it will automatically fill your damaged tire with enough air and sealant to let you drive to a safe place to fix the flat. With a cost between four and ten dollars, everyone should carry a can in the trunk. This type of product is widely available at service stations, automotive parts houses, even K-Mart and WalMart. Every car in your household should be equipped with an emergency kit, and "Flat Fix."

Some drivers exercise universal signs of distress when stranded on the highways, like lifting your vehicle hood, tying a white cloth on your antenna, or putting "Help" signs in the window. Be careful!

Remember that the highways of America can be dangerous. Lifting a hood, tying a flag on an antenna, or displaying a distress sign in the window is like waving a red flag to the highway robber...Hello! Here I am, defenseless! Come and get me! Be aware, stay alert, and use your cell phone as your first option. Flag a passing patrol car. Use "Flat Fix." If you have a CB radio, call channel 9, react. This is a national volunteer group that monitors the radio and offers road conditions, directions, and notifies emergency personnel when a driver needs help.

Chapter One Vehicle/Travel Security

REACT: Radio Emergency Associated Communication Teams
The REACT organization is a highly regarded group of volunteers that are operational in every state in America. Comprised of private radio operators, they serve travelers and their communities alike with a nationwide network of emergency and non-emergency radio operators. Members are committed to improving the safety and well being of their communities by monitoring two-way communications around the clock.

REACT teams have been very effective and well received at special events like, parades, marathons, bike events, races, and festivals, to name only a few. During emergency conditions like forest fires, chemical spills, train derailments, floods and hurricanes, they have been invaluable and have saved many lives. Because of these efforts and the work they have done with the Red Cross, Law Enforcement, FEMA, and many others, REACT was the recipient of the prestigious President's Volunteer Action Award, and numerous state and local recognition certificates of achievement.

Many REACT teams monitor Channel 9 nationwide, in the interest of public safety. Many also use radios called General Mobile Radio Service (GMRS) and have access to local GMRS Repeaters, usually on the 462.675 MHz frequencies.

I mention this because many travelers have CB radios, built-in or portable, and this information provides another option to your driving safety. If you would like more information on REACT, you can contact them at the following:

REACT International, Inc.
5210 Auth Rd. #403
Suitland, Maryland 20746
Tel. (301) 316-2900   Fax (301) 316-2903
E-Mail: react@reactintl.org

TIPS FOR THE ROAD

- The best precaution is to travel with a family member or a friend. You reduce your downside risk substantially with more than one person in the vehicle. Remember, more often than not, the bad guys pick and choose their victims. They want what you have, and have no morality when it comes to robbing or assaulting you, but they generally look for a passive prospect. Two or more people can make his job difficult. Think like the thief and you can often defeat him. The majority of roadside crimes are crimes of opportunity. These individuals are not unlike predators, always alert for a helpless target. The weaker and more defenseless the prey, the better. Don't let yourself become an easy target. Be a Hard Target.

During 1998, *52% of travelers were concerned about highway crime. Of those, 44 percent avoided traveling after dark, and 48 percent avoided traveling alone.
*Bureau of Justice Statistics, 1999

- Always plan your travel itinerary, and give an outline to a business associate or family member. Keep in touch with that person as your trip progresses. Notify them when you reach your destination.

- Use an auto club to plan your trip. You can pre-schedule your hotel accommodations and obtain valuable information on road conditions and weather before you leave. If you vary from your scheduled route, or stop somewhere other than on your scheduled itinerary, let your travel plan holder know your whereabouts. If you encounter severe weather, dangerous road conditions, become lost, or feel that you are being followed, exit the highway for the first available public area that can offer assistance.

- If you are currently under a doctor's orders for prescriptions, make sure you have a sufficient amount for your trip, allowing for unexpected delays and the name of a secondary doctor at your destination. Check for additional travel and medication advice with your doctor.

- ❏ Be especially alert to the potential for carjacking.

ROAD RAGE

Although some would argue that the subject of road rage is not appropriate for this forum, and better left for abnormal physiological, social behavior studies, I disagree for two reasons:

1. Road rage is a criminal act; either verbal abuse, or physical abuse, and a crime.
2. Road rage, left to social study experts and academia, would, for the most part, go unread by the general public...the very people who need this information.

Anger is a universal human emotion. You do not have to be a criminal to demonstrate anger. Anger, although pervasive in many criminals, lies just under the surface in most law-abiding citizens, male and female, adult or child. Sometimes we express it outwardly, but more often we tend to keep this emotion boiling and raging inside of us. This is when the pressure builds to the point of explosion. In many, hidden anger is always there in our day-to-day activities. Like a loaded gun with a hair trigger, that has no safety, a potential for disaster. It can discharge at the slightest provocation, imagined or real. If these emotions are not addressed, those deep-rooted angers will simply grow unchecked while clouding logical thought.

For many, the slightest traffic errors are conceived as a direct affront, and can reduce anger-filled drivers to blathering, uncompromising idiots. It is somewhat like a baby that cannot have his way, and reacts with a temper tantrum. They respond with anger to anything that goes against what they want and what they don't understand, or what gets in their way. That lack of interference tolerance is often the trigger to rage.

Many times road rage begins with a pretended anger to get what we want. But if that person is not taken seriously, what began as contrived anger will quickly turn into a potentially dangerous situation, and often with deadly consequences. This reaction is like a dog when someone comes too close to his food. If he is not left alone, he will bite. Simple facial expressions, driving postures and even vague gestures will elicit a deep growl, and if not checked, the boiling anger spills over.

Although many comprehensive studies have been done on the subject of road rage, and while most authorities agree that this is of growing concern, stopping it from happening is not a very practical approach to the problem. On the other hand, managing someone that is acting out his or her anger behind the wheel of a vehicle is considered the best option to a very complicated social phenomenon. I have reviewed countless articles from law enforcement agencies on this subject, spoke with, and read studies conducted by anger management organizations, and researched road studies in the Federal Government Crime Victims programs. However, the Road Rage Study, by The AAA Auto Club South of Tampa, Florida seems to sum up what most crime prevention advocates try to convey, and I feel it is very good information, and well done.

As the study points, there are good ways to handle a confrontation, and bad ways. That holds true in all situations of criminal confrontation. The following suggestions for road rage survival may keep you from harm's way, and that is why I believe it belongs in this publication. Most road rage is manageable, but it takes good information to make good decisions. Read this section aloud to your family and loved ones.

As our roadways become more congested, our lives become more complicated, and stress breeds frustration and anger. Only a thin red line separates calm reasoning from the temporary insanity of road rage. These drivers can commit incredible acts of violence – including assault and murder. When the AAA Foundation for

Traffic Safety studied more than 10,000 incidents of violent aggressive driving committed between 1990 through 1996, it found that at least 218 people were killed and another 12,610 injured when drivers allowed anger to rule over reason.

Although many of these drivers were men between the ages of 18 and 26, anyone can become angry if they let their anger take precedence over safe driving. The AAA Foundation study found that men, women, and people of all ages often drove aggressively if they were in the wrong mood or circumstances. What's more, when drivers explained the reasons they became violent, those "reasons" were often incredibly trivial:

"She wouldn't let me pass," "They kept tailgating me," or as this one driver accused of murder explained, "He practically ran me off the road – what was I supposed to do?" How can you avoid being a victim of road rage? While you can never be 100% safe, these basic guiding principles can help reduce your downside risk of becoming a victim.

When surveys asked drivers what angers them most, the results are remarkably consistent. A few specific behaviors seem unusually likely to enrage other drivers. You can protect yourself by avoiding them.

CUTTING OFF: When you merge, make sure you have plenty of room. Use your turn signals to show your intentions before making a move. If you make a mistake, or cut someone off, try to apologize to the other driver with an appropriate gesture. If someone cuts you off, slow down and give him or her room to merge into your lane.

DRIVING SLOWLY IN THE LEFT LANE: If you are in the left lane and someone wants to pass, move over and let him or her pass. You may be "in the right" because you are traveling at the speed limit, but you may also be putting yourself in danger by making drivers behind you angry. In many states and provinces, the law requires you to travel in the right lane and use the far lane only for passing.

TAILGATING: Drivers get angry when they are followed too closely. Allow at least a two-second space between your car and the car ahead. (When you see the car pass a fixed point, you should be able to count "one thousand, two thousand" before you pass that point). If you think, another car is driving too slowly and you are unable to pass, pull back and allow more space, not less. That way, if the car does something unexpected, you will have time to get out of the way. You should be able to see the headlights of the car behind you in your rearview mirror. If you feel you are being followed too closely, signal and pull over to allow the other driver go by.

GESTURES: Almost nothing makes the other driver angrier than an obscene gesture. Keep your hands on the wheel. Avoid making any gesture that might anger another driver, even "harmless" expressions of irritation like shaking your head. Be a cautious and courteous driver. Signal every time to merge or change lanes, and whenever you turn. Use your horn rarely, if ever. If you and another driver see a parking place at the same time, let that person have it. If another driver seems eager to get in front of you, "be my guest" becomes your automatic response and you won't be as offended by the other driver's rudeness.

DON'T ENGAGE: One angry driver can't start a fight unless another driver is willing to join in. You can protect yourself against aggressive drivers by refusing to become angry with them. Orator Robert Ingersoll said, "Anger blows out the lamp of the mind." A person that is angry can do things they may regret, and that includes you. If you are tempted to retaliate against another driver, think to yourself, *"Would I want to fly in an airplane whose pilot is acting like this?"* Think about what kind of a crash your anger could cause. Then cool down and continue your trip.

STEER CLEAR: Give angry driver lots of room. A driver you may have offended can "snap" and become truly dangerous. If the other driver tries to pick a fight, put as much distance between your vehicle and the other car, and then get away as quickly as possible. Do not, under any circumstances, pull off to the side of the road and try to settle things "man to man."

AVOID EYE CONTACT: If another driver is acting angry with you, don't make eye contact. Looking and staring at another driver can turn an impersonal encounter between two vehicles into a personal duel. And once things get personal, the situation can get out of hand fast. If things do escalate use your cell phone to call the police. Otherwise, drive to a place where there are people around, such as a police station, convenience store, shopping center, or even a hospital. Use your horn to get someone's attention. This will usually discourage an aggressor. Do not get out of your car. Do not go home.

ADJUST YOUR ATTITUDE: The most important actions you can take to avoid aggressive driving takes place inside your head. By changing your approach to driving, you can make every trip more pleasant. Try these ideas for a pleasant change.

FORGET WINNING: For too many motorists, driving becomes a contest. Are you one of those drivers that allow the shortest possible time for a trip and then races the clock?
If something happens to slow you down, do you get angry? The solution: Allow more time for your trip. You'll be amazed at how much more relaxed you will feel with a few extra minutes. So, instead of trying to make "good time," try to make "time good." Listen to soothing music, or a book on tape. Practice relaxation techniques, such as deep breathing. You will arrive much calmer, fresher, and in a less stressed-out frame of mind.

PUT YOURSELF IN THE OTHER DRIVER'S SHOES: Instead of judging the other driver, try to imagine why he or she is driving that way. Someone speeding and constantly changing lanes may be a volunteer fireman, or a physician rushing to a hospital. Someone who jerks from one lane to another may have a medical problem, or a crying baby. Whatever the reason, it has nothing to do with you. Stay cool and don't take other driver's actions personally.

IF YOU THINK YOU HAVE A PROBLEM, ASK FOR HELP: Courses in anger management have been shown to reduce heart attacks. These same techniques can also help angry drivers. Drivers who successfully "reinvent" their approach to the road report dramatic changes to attitude and behavior. Look for anger management courses in your area. Self-help books on stress reduction and anger management can also be helpful. Violent, aggressive driving is clearly on the rise. But you can avoid becoming a victim by using these tips provided by AAA. In the process, you may find that driving has become a completely new and more enjoyable experience.

CHAPTER TWO

Carjacking

"Expecting a carjacker, rapist or drug pusher to care that his possession or use of a gun is unlawful is like expecting a terrorist to care that his car bomb is taking up two parking spaces."
- Joseph T. Crew

The US Department of Justice Press Release, March 7, 1999 *Reports from the U.S. Department of Justice shows almost 49,000 Non-Fatal carjackings during 1998.* A weapon of some type was used in 83% of all carjackings. Of the completed carjackings, approximately 23% resulted in injuries to victims, as did 10% of the attempted carjackings.

Carjacking is defined as a completed or attempted robbery of a motor vehicle by a stranger to the victim. It differs from motor vehicle theft because the victim is present and the offender uses or threatens to use force. (BJS 1999)

- Be especially vigilant for suspicious activity around bus, train, and airport-parking areas, as FBI Crime Reports indicate 40 percent of carjackings occurred in those areas. Those same reports shows that 22% of carjackings occurred in parking lots of stores, restaurants, gas stations, and office buildings.

In carjacking incidences researched from 1997 through 1998 by the *U.S. Department of Justice, National Crime Victimization Survey,* most carjackings involving children occurred during the day. Half were at service stations, supermarkets, or shopping centers; the other half was on the street or in parking lots.

INDEPENDENCE, MISSOURI

Motorists watched in horror as a stolen vehicle sped down a highway, dragging to death a little boy who was entangled in a seatbelt outside one of the doors. Police said the car was taken when the child's mother left the child unattended, and the keys in the ignition, while she went inside a sandwich shop.
- Associated Press 1999

WHY IS CARJACKING A POPULAR CRIME?

Instead of entering into the abstract theories and sociological analysis of a criminal act, I prefer to leave the heavy thinking to the professional criminologist, and stick with what I do know about the criminal and his methods; that is what this book is all about. I am going to introduce various ways to reduce your chances of becoming a victim of crime and violence, without making you study for a master's degree in criminology. Actually, the same person with a master's degree will use the same information to keep himself out of harm's way, but he will just have a better understanding of why the guy has targeted him, and why he became a criminal. We do not need to know that…it is enough to know that he exists, to know his basic methods, and have good enough information to develop a plan that works better than his plan. Do not get confused with social cause and effect. Remember, when you are up to your butt in alligators, it is hard to remember your main objective was to drain the swamp.
Here are some of the basic reasons that carjacking is becoming a growth criminal industry.

❑ Carjacking is easy and profitable. Most carjackings are carried out under authority of lethal force, or by strong-arm tactics, but

Chapter Two — Carjacking

not before the target has been selected, and a plan of attack is in place. Remember that the bad guy always has a plan to rob you, while we, on the other hand, often fail to plan not to be robbed. Hello? It's time to wake up!

- Sometimes they carjack your vehicle by violence and force to escape a police pursuit. They have no interest in your vehicle other than a means of escaping from their pursuers. They don't want your money, and they don't want you, they just want to get away from someone that's chasing them. Under these circumstances, do not argue, give them the vehicle and get out of the line of fire as fast as possible. If someone is fleeing the police, desperation and fear of capture will often result in irrational action, and things can escalate to the danger zone very rapidly. You don't want to be there.

- Carjacking is often employed to obtain a vehicle to use in a robbery, and later abandon, or to switch vehicles after committing a crime. Do whatever it takes to get out of the vehicle. They do not need you to take your vehicle, but they might want you as a hostage, or even worse, they may not want to leave any witnesses. Most experts agree…Get out of the car!

- Carjacking for profit is somewhat less dangerous. They are most often in the carjacking business strictly to make money, and they only want your vehicle to sell for parts and profit. Major charges like kidnapping or murder is the kind of problems they don't need, nor do they want. Being considered somewhat more professional, your chances of serious injury are considerably less…most of the time.

Each year, thieves target over 200,000 vehicles for export, and sneak them across borders, or ship them overseas. Los Angeles, California leads the nation with over 60,000 vehicle thefts each year – National Insurance Crime Bureau Report 1999.

A teenage carjacker is dangerous because he is unpredictable, non-professional, often on drugs, a thrill seeker or gang member, and may simply regard carjacking as a rite of passage or status symbol. Teens and young adults commit more violent crimes than adult offenders do. Physical and sexual crimes are also common with youthful offenders. Because of lax sentencing guidelines, liberal judges, and political agendas that are far removed from punishment, criminally minded teens are not concerned with being held accountable for their actions, and all too often it is a bazaar and sometimes-deadly game. Do not try to lecture or take an authoritative posture with this type of thief. That may only enflame the perpetrator. Get out of his face as fast as possible. You can replace your car, but not your life. Under the right circumstances, that cherub-faced teen can be a real monster. Don't misunderstand me, there are far more good, young people than bad...but when they go rotten, they often go rotten to the core - as mean as a junkyard dog, comes to mind.

- Sophisticated vehicle alarm systems, improved door locks, effective anti theft devices, *(I will talk more on these products later)* and more communities taking a pro-active approach toward stopping the car thief, are making it more difficult to steal a car. Traditional car theft is far more common than carjacking, but some thieves perceive carjacking as easier. They simply walk up on your blind side, grab hold, and jerk you out of your vehicle. A simple but effective plan. With more violent action movies painting this crime as "exciting," it continues to grow in popularity. Be aware of your environment, establish a comfort zone, develop a personal safety strategy drawn from the information you find in this book, and you can defeat a carjacker. You don't have to be a defenseless victim.

- In some high crime areas, carjacking is a way of obtaining wheels for a drive-by shooting, or to transact a drug deal, or to commit a robbery. It hides the thief's identity, keeps his own vehicle safe from identification, and lets him travel to his destination with relative anonymity.

COMMON CARJACKING METHODS

- **ARMED CARJACKING**: Based on *U.S. Department of Justice Crime Reports*, a weapon of some type is used in over 80 percent of all carjackings. Therefore, it will come as no great surprise when I tell you that the method of choice is to walk up on unsuspecting drivers, stick a firearm in their face and take the vehicle. Simple and to the point. "Get out of the car or I will blow your brains all over the dashboard." Not exactly Academy Award™ material, just effective dialog that gets the job done. These guys have been doing it the same way for a long time... If it's not broke, why fix it? **(BJS) Carjacking in the United States, NJC 171145)**

- **INTENTIONAL ACCIDENTS**: One carjack ploy is for a team of two or more to intentionally cause a minor accident. When you exit your vehicle to inspect the damage, a team member will jump into your car and drive away. Often this staged fender-bender will be at an isolated location that offers concealment for one of the team members, and provides easy access to a freeway or arterial highway. Not rocket science, but it is a plan. Do you have a plan to stop it?

- **SERVICE STATIONS/CONVENIENCE STORES:** Self-service pumps are made to order for the carjacker. We frequently leave the keys in the ignition while filling the tank, and then walk to the store to pay the bill. Dah! What is wrong with this picture? Even if we pay at the pump, we are prime targets for carjacking, motor vehicle theft, robbery, purse snatching, or worse. I often wonder if a carjacker came up with the idea of self-service pumps. They seem to be the perfect place for all manners of pillage and plunder.

- **STOP LIGHTS:** Because so many of us fail to lock all of our car doors, a stop light is like a drive up valet service for the carjacker. Considering the fact that almost everyone tailgates one another, we are blocked in traffic, and cannot get away. As the late Jackie Gleason used to say, "How sweet it is." Even locking the doors is not the magic cure-all as vehicle safety glass is designed to shatter quite easily. It sometimes seems like all of the cards are stacked in favor of the bad guy…I assure you, they are not. Using some of the defense strategies that are in this book could tilt those odds in your favor by a wide margin.

- **PUBLIC PARKING:** Parking garages and parking lots are fertile hunting grounds for carjackers. Beware of phony lot attendants and bogus valet parking staff.

This is only a sampling of carjacking methodology. Don't let yourself underestimate any criminal mind. They can be very creative when it comes to separating you from your vehicle, or any other type crime they attempt. It has been said that if you think like a criminal, you can often defeat one. However, the people most often suggesting this course of action are crime prevention specialists, or law enforcement personnel. They work and study issues of criminal cause and effect for a living, and the transition of thinking as an honest citizen, to walking in the shoes of a thief, is a simple training exercise for them. Yes, in some circumstances you can think like a thief, and often deter a crime from happening, or escalating. However, it has been my experience that most honest citizens have not the foggiest idea of the depth and scope of the criminal's mind, his methods, or the danger he represents. The closest most average people have been to a criminal act of violence is television, the movies, or a fiction novel (excluding war, which is violent by nature, but not in the context of a criminal nature that we are addressing). The honest person's mind is simply different than that of the criminal. Therefore, without some training in this area, John Q. Citizen cannot walk in the shoes of the thief. That, in a nutshell, is why he is easy to victimize. His bachelor's degree in computer science, his years of studying to become a doctor, the discipline exercised to earn his or her teaching credentials, or the satisfaction of becoming a master plumber, have done nothing to prepare him for a walk in the shoes of a criminal. This is the reason the Federal government, state and city law enforcement organizations, including the private sector, are spending billions of dollars on various crime prevention programs. Crime and violence is simply too costly to ignore. The credit section of this book will list many of the organizations and programs for your review.

The most recent study by the *Justice Department's Bureau of Justice statistics (BJS)* found that almost 3% of the nation's adult population, or about 1 in every 34 adults was incarcerated, on probation, or on parole at the end of 1999. That means 5.9 million adult men and women are in confinement or on some form of federal, state, or local supervision, and classified as criminals…and folks, that is not even counting the youth offenders.

When these people are incarcerated in prisons, short term or long, what do you think the number one conversation they have with each other is? They all have one thing in common …they talk about their crime. They do not talk about problems of education, employment, and alcohol and drug abuse, unless a caseworker, parole officer, or the Judge is within hearing range, but they do talk about how they were busted! Moreover, they will spend countless hours, days, months, and even years analyzing what went wrong, and learning how to do it better the next time. This nation's jails and prisons are finishing schools for crime and violence. The professors are the best of the worst that America has to offer. I say all this to preface my point; never underestimate any criminal mind. The psychologist and criminologists believe that they can analyze a pattern of attitudes and behavior, and reduce the threat of crime. With this lofty goal in mind, they can then develop an environment where crime cannot flourish and grow. I hope the experts are on the right track, and I personally believe it is worthy of support, but this is not the platform to launch that rocket. We are going to stay our course, and remain focused on things we can do, right now, to protect ourselves from becoming a victim.

Justice Department (BJS) REF. 202/307/0784

RESISTANCE

- If you are confronted by a carjacker armed with a **firearm**, do exactly what you are told, try to avoid verbal and physical confrontations, and if he tells you to get out of the car, get out as fast as possible. **Do not** greet the carjacker with an attitude. **Do not** argue. Do **not** become defensive. **Do not** say anything. Just get out, leave the keys in the ignition, and then put as much distance between you and the vehicle as fast as possible. If he said he wants your car, chances are, that is what he wants…give it to him! If he tells you to stay in the car it is then time for you to consider extreme measures for survival. Take your chances right there instead of some remote secondary crime scene. He doesn't need you in the car to rob you, or take your car. Most experts agree that staying with the carjacker cuts your probability for survival drastically. Statistics show there is a 98% chance you will not survive if you stay with the carjacker. If you refuse his demands to stay in the car and run away there is a very high rate of survival. If you have a child in the car, tell him he can have your vehicle but not your child, and then take your child out of the car and walk away. Leave your purse or wallet to distract the thief. Try to keep a good mental picture of the carjacker for later police investigation, but do not make that obvious. First order of business, get out of dodge!

Aside from our homes, a car is probably the second biggest financial investment we make. With this in mind and understanding that many automobile owners become very attached to their vehicles, it is no wonder they often become defensive when someone damages or tries to take this hard earned property. If the carjacker has no visible signs of deadly force, and is attempting to take your vehicle by strong-arm or intimidation methods, your response then becomes a matter of personal judgment. You know your abilities better than anyone else. If you do decide to resist, it must be carried out swiftly and decisively. Recent Justice Department report show 62% of all carjacking victims took some type of action to defend themselves or their property. While 34 percent of victims used non-confrontational responses, 19 percent confronted the attacker by attacking the offender, chasing, or trying to capture him. You have the right to protect yourself and your property. How you do that must always conform to the rules of law. As crime in general continue to increase in violence, and individuals, businesses, homeowners, and communities take a more proactive approach to crime prevention, many citizens are looking more closely at various self-defense options. The growing popularity of self-defense classes, guard dogs, and firearms has a positive side and a negative side. On the positive side, it shows people are becoming more aware, and they are now beginning to think about responding to the problem instead of simply reacting to the problem. A pro-active position is growing in popularity. On the negative side the issues of crime and victims is complicated, and seemingly easy solutions like martial arts, guard dogs, or firearms is not only simplistic, but in most cases, it creates more liability than protection. Developing a personal safety strategy with a foundation built on awareness and avoidance, on the other hand, can serve you well, while keeping your liability at a minimum. Your choice of non-confrontation through awareness and avoidance planning is far safer than a Karate kick; a pit bull named Kujo, or a round from a .357 Magnum, all of which have great liability. To make matters more frustrating, in many situations, those remedies would be considered unlawful force and illegal. The law says you have the right to defend yourself, but you can only use lethal force if confronted by lethal force.

Before you think it, let me say it, "I'd rather be tried by twelve than carried by six." I can understand this attitude of frustration, but you do not have to find yourself in court defending your actions if you develop a sensible strategy not to be a victim. Besides, you probably would not like your cellmate, Bubba, and you would definitely not like the coffee. So let's set the hard line attitude aside and let common sense dictate to our needs.

INTENTIONAL ACCIDENT PLAN

- You may not be able to avoid **intentional accidents**, but you can survive them. If you are in a minor fender-bender, and you suspect foul play, do not stop. First, you will need to do a few things. Make sure that all your doors are locked and your windows are up. Signal the other driver that you know he bumped you, and there is a problem, but you are not going to stop right where you are. You can do this by waving to him and motioning him to follow you. Turn on your four-way flashers and drive slowly. If you have a cell phone (and you should), call the police and inform them of your situation. Do not hang up. Continue driving until you reach a public place. Let the dispatcher know where you are, follow instructions. If the other driver stops when you do, tell him you have called the police, and then remain in your locked vehicle until they arrive. If it was an attempted carjacking, chances are he will be long gone the moment you signaled and got on the cell phone. A good description of the car and a license number will make the investigating officer's day.

SERVICE STATION/CONVENIENCE STORE PLAN

- Most carjackings at **service stations and convenience stores** are crimes of opportunity. You are preoccupied putting air in a tire, gassing up, or have left your keys in the ignition and went inside to pay, and then they strike. Be aware of your surroundings at all times. Do not leave keys in a vehicle unless you are in there with them. Report any suspicious activity to the clerk or attendant. Do not talk to strangers. If faced with an armed situation, be respectful of the danger. If someone demands your car or keys, use your best judgment...I would give them the keys and get out of there as fast as possible, or at the very least, get out of arm's reach. Most professionals would advise cooperation and non-aggression. Make note of the approximate height, weight, clothing and any identifiable marks or scars. This guy needs to be in jail!

STOP LIGHT/STOP SIGN PLAN

- **Stoplights** and **stop signs** are great for regulating traffic, but they can be deadly traps when used by carjackers. Watch for anyone loitering or acting suspicious when you stop. Make sure your doors are always locked while driving, and never leave a passenger door window rolled down. If someone on foot becomes aggressive or threatening, start honking your horn. If the person tries to force his way into the car, drive through the light or stop sign. If you turn with the traffic flow, this will lessen your chance of an accident. Many experts believe an accident if preferable to this guy gaining access to your car. Taking your car is one thing, taking you along with your car is something far more frightening, and statistically speaking, carries a very low rate of survival.

- Never tailgate. This practice can set you up for carjacking. If you are blocked in, with a two-man carjacking team, one can quickly break your window and get in the passenger or driver's side, or if your door is unlocked, he can pull you out and drive off. The perpetrator will not care about damaging another car, or your being injured in the process. They want your vehicle, and are going to do whatever it takes to get it. A good defensive practice is to leave yourself enough room to quickly drive around the car in front of you if escape becomes necessary. If he gains access to the passenger side or back seat, and orders you to drive off, it's time to pull a D B Cooper, and bail out! Leave your keys in the ignition, open your door and dive out and down away from the car. Then run as fast as your little legs will allow. He now has the keys, the car, and your purse. That should be enough to appease him while you concentrate on escape and evasion. A life for a car and a purse? Not a bad trade.

PARKING LOT/GARAGE PLAN

Public parking lots need to be given careful consideration. Most are good, safe places to park, but there are many parking lots that should award you with a Medal of Valor, or a Combat Service Ribbon for surviving the ordeal. Always try to use attended parking lots, but do not automatically assume the attendant is trustworthy. Don't let the sign "Bonded & Insured" lull you into a false sense of security. It usually only covers vehicle damage and has nothing to do with a dishonest attendant. Your best bet is Park and Lock facilities, where you can lock valuables in the trunk, and keep the keys. If there is an attendant on the lot, park as close to him as possible. If not, park in a well lit area. Be cautious entering and leaving. Look around. Be aware! If it is a multilevel garage, do not use the stairwells. Don't get on the elevator with a stranger. If you want to walk, use the auto ramp; just be careful of traffic. If you have to run, you have two directions to go, if you find it necessary to scream, it carries nicely, and you have good visibility all around. By the way, if you are female, carry lightweight tennis shoes; do not try running from an assailant in high heals. If the parking garage is part of a shopping mall, or department store, ask the security guard to escort you. They love that macho stuff, and that is part of their job. Be especially alert to someone loitering or following you. If you feel in danger, return to the store. If you are still in your car, leave, and tell the attendant.

SIMPLE REMINDERS

- Do not let apathy make you a statistic.
- Establish your own comfort zone, and do not let anyone in **your** space.

- Lock your doors and windows immediately after entering or exiting your vehicle.
  1. If you lock your doors, you reduce your chances of becoming a carjack or auto theft victim by 60%.
  2. If you roll up your windows, your loss reduction is 20%.
  3. If you remove your keys after parking your vehicle, your loss reduction is up to 80%, depending upon where you park.
- **Bureau of Justice Statistics, 1999**

- Lock your doors. Have you heard this before? Good! My plan is working! You will hear it again! Lock your doors!

Remember that a carjacking takes only 15 to 20 seconds to complete. If you respond inappropriately, the results can last a lifetime.

- Keep your doors locked and windows rolled up (yes, I do repeat this often…because I care about you!).
- Be aware. Stop, look, and listen.
- Do not become complacent.
- Carjacking is a crime of opportunity and has nothing to do with race, color, or sex.
- Look around before getting in your car.
- Be cautious of strangers asking for directions.
- Keep your windows rolled up.
- Do not stop to offer roadside assistance. Call by telephone to send help.
- Carjackers are usually armed.
- If you are forced by armed carjacker to drive, some survival experts suggest, as an option of last resort, crashing your car off the road, if you have a driver's side air bag. Let's hope the carjacker does not have the same protection.
- Trust your instincts. Most of the time, they serve us well. Watch for opportunities to escape your abductor.

Chapter Two   Carjacking

In *Tallahassee, Florida, on February 5, 1996*, a motorist gambled on his driver's side air bag, and won. Hijacked by two teenage carjackers, who forced him at gunpoint to drive, and in fear for his life, he crashed his vehicle into the back of a truck. One carjacker survived and was introduced to the Florida prison system, the carjacker in the front seat died.

Creative thinking, a cool composure, and a good air bag probably saved the car owner's life. Did I mention bravery? This may not be the most appropriate option, but it is an option. The reasons for this radical decision are not known, but clearly he did what he felt was warranted by the circumstances. If I had a gun to my head, felt my murder was imminent; an option of last resort might not be a bad idea. This, of course, can only be a decision made by the hostage.

Another example of creative survival techniques: **In New York City a person that was carjacked and placed in the trunk of the car was able to pull the wires out of the vehicle taillights, thus attracting police, and subsequently was saved.**

God forbid, you should ever find yourself in the trunk of your vehicle; you now have another option in your crime survival arsenal. This is a great example of my earlier statement: You have to have good information to make good decisions. Do you have to know what wires are for the taillights? No. Tear them all out!

Don't take the subject of carjacking lightly. *The U.S. Bureau of Justice Statistics data, during 1992-1996* pointed out that approximately 49,000 carjacking attempts were successful each of those years, and injuries were reported in 23%. However, no data on murders by carjackers was available. They did interview over 400,000 victims over the age of twelve, but only **survivors** could be interviewed.
*In 1999, The U.S. Supreme Court turned aside a challenge that would have weakened the anti-carjacking law that makes it a federal crime to steal a car "with intent to cause death or serious

bodily injuries" to the car's driver. We are winning the war on carjacking and other crimes, but ever so slowly. It is a frustrating achievement when we know that in the next 21 seconds a violent crime will occur in America.

*CNN March 2, 1999

Although carjacking has captured the headlines nationwide, statistically, your chances of becoming a carjack victim are very slim, and good preventive measures can reduce that risk even further. As this crime continues to grow in popularity, memorizing the rule of six will greatly reduce your chance of finding yourself in harm's way.

CARJACKING OPPORTUNITY KNOCKS: (Rule of six)
1. Stop lights and controlled intersections
2. Garages, parking lots, shopping malls
3. Self-service gas stations
4. ATM's (automatic teller machines)
5. Residential driveways
6. Highway entry and exit ramps

Carjacking is growing in popularity, but it is not a "new" crime, by any stretch of the imagination. We were first introduced to the term "carjacking" in the late 70's by the news media pointing out a different type of violent car theft hitting our inner cities. Violence sells newspapers. Starting with the media, then catching the attention of film producers and television writers, it was not very long before the copycat syndrome took hold and carjacking rapidly became a household word. For many, it is the preferred method of car theft. The thief does not have to bypass complicated and noisy car alarms, sophisticated, integrated ignition switches, and state of the art wheel locking devices. Just stick a gun in the driver's face and take possession of the vehicle in seconds, intact, keys and all. If he has no firearm, he simply targets easier victims; female, elderly, or handicapped, physically drags them out and drives off.

Can we put the blame for this violent and often deadly crime on the media, movies, and over creative writers? Of course not. Crime is a complex by-product of our cultural building blocks, the social DNA I mentioned earlier. Cause and effect is directly tied to political, legal, economic, demographic, technological and social forces that make our society what it is. Is it getting better? In my opinion, yes! Does it have a simple fix? No. I know enough about sociological and criminology issues to realize they cannot provide a definitive blueprint for change, but you can take some comfort in knowing that thousands of very knowledgeable and caring people are working on solutions as we speak. However, until better answers are found, and fixes are in place, this book does offer some options to reduce our chances of becoming a victim. I doubt that preventive measures will ever achieve one hundred percent effectiveness, but you do not have to make it easy for the carjacker.

GET INVOLVED

Practice good citizenship by working with law enforcement, auto clubs, and your neighborhood watch program. Take the initiative! Compile information about carjacking from this book, and others, and make an informational flyer for distribution in your neighborhood.
➢ Ask the local Community Service Officer to help develop a factual brochure on carjacking (you have my permission to use information from this publication for a project of this nature).
➢ Ask to speak at the local Driver Education Program on the subject of carjacking, and pass out flyers for the class.
➢ Send an information flyer to local parking lots for distribution.
➢ Carjacking brochures could be a project for your local scout groups. Distribute handouts at garages, service stations, retail shops, etc.
➢ Ask a printer to provide door hangers as a public service. Let him put his name and address on the flyers.
Whenever a citizen takes a stand to improve the quality of life in the community, other will always rally to the cause. Taking a

proactive approach to these problems will serve as a magnet to attract others that are sick and tired of crime and violence, in any form. When a grass root movement gathers momentum, it is an awesome force for change.

CHAPTER THREE

Auto and Property Theft

"Things aren't right. If a burglar breaks into your home and you shoot him, he can sue you. For what, restraint of trade?"
—*Bill Maher, 1993 on Politically Incorrect*

"The world is a dangerous place to live, not because of the people who are evil, but because of the people who don't do anything about it." – *Albert Einstein*

Auto theft, as well as property theft from a vehicle, is a growth industry that is alive and well throughout the world, but the United States leads the industrial world in this category. Auto theft and auto burglaries are low risk and profitable.

Not only is there a growing demand for expensive automobile parts, but contents like laptop computers, sophisticated electronic gadgets, and personal items like luggage and credit cards, means easy picking for thieves. It is a huge business! Trust me, your car is a target for thieves as you read this publication. While we will never be able to make ourselves 100% safe from vehicle theft, we can do something to cut our downside risk. Awareness and education are the keys.

A general description of vehicle theft (it could vary from state to state) is any person who drives or takes a vehicle that he or she

Chapter Three   Auto and Property Theft

does not own, without the consent of the owner. Said person has intent to either temporarily or permanently deprive the owner thereof of his or her title to or possession of the vehicle, whether with or without intent to steal the vehicle. This also applies to any person who is party to or an accomplice in the driving or unauthorized taking or stealing, and is in violation of the public offense of motor vehicle theft, a felony. Lawyer talk for…"You dirty rat, you stole my car!"

Based on available crime statistics released by the *FBI Uniformed Crime Report, and other crime trend monitors, a motor vehicle is stolen every 17 seconds in the United States. It might be noted that crime statistics vary from year to year, but this represents the most current data available.

- Establish a locked door policy. *Annually there are over 1.2 million thefts of contents and more than 1.4 million thefts of accessories from vehicles nationwide. There is a more serious side of vehicle theft. If you happen on a theft in progress, it can quickly escalate into a more serious crime, sometimes with deadly consequences.

*U.S. Department of Justice Press Release 2/7/99

- Keep everything of value in your trunk. If you do leave personal items or other articles in the car, make sure they are out of sight.

- Never leave your keys in the ignition.

- Establish a locked door policy, even in front of your home.

- Mark all property such as radios, radar detectors (Caution! In some states it is illegal to use radar detectors), cell phones, cameras, and other portable items with an identification number. Many police departments will loan you an engraver to mark these items. Use your driver's license number, and not your Social Security Number. Keep an inventory of the personal items you travel with. This can be helpful in a police investigation, and support any insurance claims you might submit.

- Make a wallet copy of your tag number and Vehicle Identification (VIN) Number.

- Keep the home keys and vehicle keys separate.

- When parking, try to leave your vehicle in well-lit areas. Avoid using unattended parking lots for long periods. Leave **only** your ignition key with a parking attendant. Keep your glove box locked. If the ignition key unlocks the glove box or console, have a locksmith re-key it to use your door keys.

- If you see a vehicle burglary in progress, or simply someone loitering around your vehicle, leave the area immediately. Do not confront the thief! Avoidance and non-confrontation are your best options. Call the police. If a burglary has already occurred, do not disturb anything as you might destroy evidence that could be used to identify the burglar. Don't touch <u>anything</u> inside or outside. Take pictures and keep copies of any police incident reports for your insurance company, or car rental agency.

- Avoid going out alone after dark.

- If you are confronted with a robbery or assault situation outside of your vehicle or in a parking lot, quickly drop down and roll under a nearby vehicle – It is <u>very</u> difficult to get someone out from under a vehicle. If you are running from an assailant or robber and think you cannot outrun him, pick a vehicle that has the most ground room. As soon as you get under the car, start screaming as you brace your foot against the undercarriage. Depending on your size, and the height of the vehicle, this escape and evasion tactic may not work, but in more cases than not it will get you out of harm's way. Incidentally, if you don't think you can get under a vehicle because it sits too low to the ground, you will be amazed at how easy it is to scramble your way into a tight place when someone just told you he was going to cut your head off. Just remember one thing about this escape and evasion tactic; make sure <u>you</u> have the keys. Lying under 3 or 4,000 pounds of automobile when a thief has the keys is not cool. This bears repeating - whatever you do, do not get in the car with the robber. He doesn't need you in the car to steal your car, or rob you. If he wants you in the car, he has another agenda that can have deadly consequences.

CAUTION – THIS EVASIVE MANEUVER SHOULD <u>NOT</u> BE ATTEMPTED IF YOU ARE CONFRONTED WITH DEADLY FORCE. WE WILL DISCUSS THE ISSUE OF DEADLY FORCE CONFRONTATION IN THE PERSONAL PROTECTION SECTION.

- Observe the surrounding area before you enter or exit your vehicle. Let your intuition work for you. If you have that tingling feeling that something is not right, use extreme caution. Those gut feelings are usually right on the mark. Turn around and go back where you came from.

- If you have burglar alarm remote with a panic button and you feel threatened, activate the alarm, even though you may not be in the car, but a short distance from it. The noise can attract attention to your situation and frighten the would-be thief into running.

REMEMBER, POTENTIALLY DANGEROUS SITUATIONS CAN BE AVOIDED OR CONTROLLED BY DILLIGENTLY PRACTICING GOOD CRIME MANAGEMENT TECHNIQUES.

- Don't leave the keys in the car. I know this sounds like a no-brainer, but according to *The Florida Anti-Car Theft Committee, 25% of stolen vehicles had the keys in them.

- Don't hide a set of keys anywhere on your vehicle. Those little magnetic key holders can work in only so many places, and the thieves know those places. Do not play that hide and seek game. You lose every time.

- Never leave your vehicle running while unattended. (In most states this is a violation of the State Law, and you can be ticketed). We have covered this issue before, but it is such a common mistake it bears repeating. The other day I went to the Post Office and saw at least three cars with the motor running, or keys in the ignition. ATM's, gas stations, convenience stores, motels and hotels, airports, dry cleaners…the list goes on. Leaving your keys in the ignition or worse, leaving the car running, becomes a variable smorgasbord for the enormous appetite of the car thieves.

If you make it easy for someone to steal your car, you cannot call yourself a victim…you can only call yourself a volunteer.

- If you drive an older vehicle, do not become complacent, and believe you will not become a target. Not only do old parts sell well, but also older vehicles make excellent low-profile robbery or drive-by shooting vehicles. Because they are easier to steal, they are often the vehicles of choice for joy riding by underage kids…a deadly highway receipt for disaster. If we leave the keys in our vehicle, contrary to state laws, and a young child takes the vehicle for a joy-ride and is in a fatal accident, you might be found criminally negligent, or defending your actions in a civil litigation. Aside from that, it would be a terrible burden to carry, knowing that simply leaving the keys in the car was indirectly responsible for the life of a child - motor vehicle theft aside.

- Photocopy your registration papers and carry them on your person. As a matter of good crime prevention, don't leave anything with your address in the glove box. If you do, and someone steals your car, especially with the keys in it, they now have your address and your house keys. It is one thing to have your car stolen but quite another to give this criminal easy access to our home and loved ones.

- If your car and car keys are stolen, have your house locks re-keyed that day! Also, change the code on your garage door opener (if personal safety and vehicle loss are not an issue with you, do you see how expensive and inconvenient lax security can become?). Do you carry the keys to your office? Your motorcycle or boat?

- Keep valuable items out of sight from predators. Leaving a purse, laptop, of shopping items is an open invitation for theft. It only takes seconds to break a window and take possession of your property. Keep all valuables in the trunk and out of sight from prying eyes. Did I mention that an ounce of prevention is worth a pound of cure? If I did, some things are worth repeating.

- Don't make it easy for bogus tow trucks to drive off with your pride and joy. Turning your wheels sharply to the right or left will make it difficult to tow. Front wheel drive vehicles should be left in reverse drive.

- If you have a garage at home...use it for your vehicle! If you lock your car in your garage, you reduce your chance of losing it to a car thief by almost 100%. The average thief wants quick access and easy escape. He is not interested in garage locked vehicles. The exception to this rule would be a burglar. A home intruder might search a car for valuables, but only in rare cases steal the vehicle.

- Anti theft devices are your best option to vehicle thieves.

- If someone is following you, drive to the nearest open business, fire station, or police station.

During 1998, 52% of residents were afraid of becoming a victim of street crime. Of those, 44% avoided certain routes and areas, 49% avoided going out at night, and 48% avoided going out alone (Bureau of Justice Statistics, 1999).

Fear is a question: What are you afraid of and why? Just as the seed of health is in illness, because illness contains information, your fears are a treasure house of self-knowledge if you explore them. - Marilyn Ferguson

CHAPTER FOUR

Anti-Theft Devices

"If you don't secure your vehicle, and someone takes it, consider yourself a co-conspirator and pat yourself on the back for a job well done." - Joseph C. Martini

Anti-theft devices are generally recognized as the best safeguard to vehicle theft and auto burglary. Even simple devices like steering wheel bar locks are a deterrent (they can also prevent air bag thefts, a popular and financially rewarding target). However, as vehicles and accessories become more expensive, the demand for a better mousetrap will continue to grow. New technology and vehicle security demands have built a multi-million dollar industry that is making car theft difficult and high risk. Unfortunately, car thieves and their buyers are also tracking these growth industries, and they are also becoming increasingly more sophisticated. To better understand the problem, the first question we must address is why vehicle theft exists. Three basic reasons come to mind: Profit, Pleasure, and Secondary use. Profit is the easiest to understand. Vehicles and parts are in demand and profitable. Many thieves take a car to sell the parts and accessories to private parties who do not care where they came from. "Honest" citizens that have no morality about placing an order with a thief simply to beat the price of retail purchasing are creating their own monster. That same thief that sells a stolen part or accessory would have no second thoughts about stealing those same parts and accessories from the same person they were sold to. It is a vicious circle. That same "honest" buyer of stolen goods is probably crying the loudest about the high cost of parts and insurance, yet is largely responsible for the problem and contributes nothing to the solution. Buying stolen property, of any kind, is illegal. If you know someone that is a buyer or seller of stolen parts or accessories, report them to the police. If you do not take a proactive stance on these issues, you can watch prices skyrocket, and insurance soar even higher. The cost of crime and violence in America is a debt we all pay for, one way or another. You are a part of the problem, or are a part of the solution, but you cannot be neutral.

A more serious concern to Law Enforcement is the professional organized crime enterprises that deal in stolen vehicles and accessories, commonly referred to as "Chop Shops." Chop Shops are often auto repair facilities, auto body shops, or wrecking yards that illegally engage in buying, disassembling, altering, reassembling, selling, or shipping and storage of stolen motor vehicles and parts. These organizations are often very sophisticated, frequently computer linked with thieves and buyers alike, and are often able alter or dispose of products too fast for authorities to track. Once a vehicle goes through the front door of a chop shop, is altered and receives counterfeit paperwork, and comes out the back, it is easily mainstreamed back into an unsuspecting public. Prevention is the best solution. If vehicle owners can affect the source with better anti-theft devices and proactive attitudes, it will not be as profitable for these enterprises to operate. I don't believe we will ever be 100 percent effective, but we do not need to make life easy for this type of crime to victimize honest citizens. Remember that crime prevention begins with personal responsibility.

Another type of vehicle theft is commonly referred to as **Joy Riding**. Taking a vehicle from a family member, someone you know, or a stranger, just to ride around and later abandon. It is still stealing. Often this seemingly victimless criminal act is committed as a prank. At other times, it is an act of juvenile mischief and in most cases can be directly tied to alcohol or drug use, or lack of parental supervision. The perpetrators are frequently under the legal age to drive, and the theft is anything but victimless.

Television and newspapers are constantly reporting the carnage caused by this type of vehicle thievery. Children barely able to see over the steering wheel, unable to maintain control, losing their lives, and the lives of others for no other reason than the thrill of stealing a car...Joy Riding. The social-psychological thinkers like to point to the lack of parental control, the breakdown of personal esteem, and that magic catchall referred to as peer pressure. We can debate this until the cows come home, but one simple fact will remain glaringly apparent, we are not practicing good crime prevention by leaving our cars vulnerable to theft, thus indirectly aiding and abetting. While we wait for the shrinks to analyze cause and effect, we should "harden" our vehicles to this type of crime. We are not dealing with professional criminals, well trained in bypassing elaborate anti-theft devices, motivated by greed and profit. I am talking about children; kids, little Billy down the street, or our own sons and daughters making bad life decisions. Because we know these crimes take place, and alluding to the fact that nobody seems to be of one mind as to why, or the best course of action to prevent it from happening, let's not make it easy for the crime to take place in the first place. Practice that locked door policy we talk so much about, don't leave keys where kids can find them, and take advantage of the wide array of anti-theft devices available on the market. It is a shame when we have to lock everything up, but nothing else seems to be working. Until we once again start instilling common sense and values in our youth, let's not make it easy for them to ruin their lives, and ours, with a criminal conviction or the mangled aftermath of a vehicle fatality. In short, let's lock up the cars...not the kids.

The third reason for vehicle theft is **secondary use**. Stealing a car to use in the commission of another crime such as robbery, burglary, transporting drugs, or drive-by shootings. These are prime reasons for using a stolen vehicle and not their own. This problem must be approached with extreme caution. This thief differs greatly from the professional car thief motivated by profit, or the Joy Rider out for a thrill. Often motivated by money, revenge or anger, they are dangerous and unpredictable, and should be dealt with accordingly.

Now that I have given you a better understanding of the criminal types that steal cars, and we have talked at some length about vehicle theft prevention, this is a good time to provide an overview of the explosion in anti-theft alarm technology. For the most part, our homes are the largest investment we will make, and our cars are the second biggest investment. Some vehicles are even more expensive than the average house. It is no wonder our cars are prime targets. As a result, the alarm business has become our first line of defense in the war on vehicle thefts. Let's face the facts; if there were no profits in vehicle theft, vehicle theft would not exist. Thieves steal things of value. The more the value, the more likely it is to be a target, and your protection level should be in direct proportion to that value. How much security do you provide for your garden hose? How much security do you provide for your car? All things are relative to cost or perceived value.

Many vehicle manufacturers provide alarm systems as standard equipment, while others offer a wide array of security options as accessories. With the staggering cost of automobiles in today's competitive marketplace, everyone agrees it is foolish to spend that kind of money without safeguarding your investment. Even insurance companies are encouraging alarm systems with a vehicle purchase. Primarily because it protects their downside risk of paying expensive auto theft claims, many states mandate insurance discounts for anti-theft devices. At last, count twelve states required insurance companies to give a discount on the comprehensive portion of your auto insurance policy if you have an alarm. The discount amount is based on the type of alarm, and the levels of protection it offers. Most are in favor of a passive-setting alarm because it arms your vehicle automatically (The more layers of protection the alarm provides, the less likely a theft will occur, and that equates into less money paid out in vehicle and content theft by the insurance industry). It would seem this is a win-win situation for all parties, and it would not surprise me if

Chapter Four   Anti-Theft Devices

this becomes common practice in all states. After all, we are **required** to carry insurance on a vehicle. We are **not** required to have alarm systems. If we spend our own money to protect the vehicle from theft, and in doing so we drastically cut the risk of the insurance carrier from sustaining a loss from auto theft, carjacking, content theft and vandalism, they should be delighted to offer some form of compensation or discount program. The insurance companies in the following states are required to pay between 5% and 25% for anti-theft systems, but many states will negotiate with the policyholder. It is a competitive business. If I pay my hard-earned money for an anti-theft device and they don't offer me a break…I'm changing carriers.

Some States that Mandate Insurance Discounts

Florida
Illinois
Kentucky
Louisiana
Massachusetts
Minnesota
New Jersey
New Mexico
New York
Pennsylvania
Rhode Island
Texas
Washington
Source: Insurance Information Institute

The biggest problem is not negotiating a fair and equitable rate, but deciding what anti-theft device to use that will give the best insurance break, yet provide the most favorable level of protection for our budget and lifestyle. We all know what we paid for our vehicles, and most of us know what we can afford to spend, but hardly anyone is prepared for the shopping nightmare of anti-theft devices. Even though I have been around the security and general home alarm industry most of my life, I was caught completely flatfooted when I started researching this growth industry. The market is changing rapidly. Remember, we are dealing with the first baby steps of a technological explosion of the computer industry, and that has a direct impact on alarm systems. As vehicles become more expensive, and the public's fascination for high technology escalates, demand is creating even more research and development. Even budgeting for a rudimentary alarm system you can expect a cost between $200 and $400, and it can escalate rapidly from there. But the real dilemma is not cost; it is understanding what it is they are offering. Remember when you purchased your first computer? Modems, CDs ROMs, Data Protocols, Zip Drives, Universal Serial Ports, Floppy Drives, CPUs, PCI Slots, Hard drives, and these were the simple things, but they were mind numbing at the time, Well the anti-theft industry is not unlike the computer retailer (and in fact, most *are* computerized devices). Walk into any alarm retail/installation facility and you are immediately hit with slick marketing hype, audio/video promotional packaging from the best marketers New York has to offer, and a mind - boggling selection and very impressive demo programs. Lights flash, horns honk, and sirens scream, as you are inundated by widgets like Immobilizers, Code-Hopping integration, Remote starters, Passive arm circuitry, Proximity sensors, Electronic scanning, Remote notification, Time delay, Ignition cutoff protocol, and this is the simple stuff. Wow! The one part of this subject I do understand...you <u>need</u> what they have to offer! Here are a few suggestions, and remember, before you make your final decision, check with your insurance company. You should be able to qualify for a healthy rate discount.

ANTI-THEFT DEVICES

Basically speaking, you can look at vehicle anti-theft protection in four levels of protection.

Level #1

Common Sense: The most cost efficient theft prevention approach is simply to never leave your keys in an unattended vehicle, and always maintain a locked door policy. This in itself is sufficient security for a very large group of thieves'…amateurs, and bad guy wannabe's, and simple joy riders.

Level # 2

Warning Devices: Visible or audible deterrents. Products like steering locking bars (The Club), visible warning decals, window etching, Watch Your Car Decals (a national anti-car theft program), and alarms with sirens or horn and lighting interfacing.

Level #3

Immobilizing Devices: Electronic Immobilizers prevent thieves from bypassing the ignition, or hot-wiring the vehicle. Computer chip ignition keys. Fuel and ignition shut-off switches. Passive Immobilizers for starters, ignition, and fuel.

Level #4

Tracking Technology: Tracking systems that are monitored by police or computer receiving stations. Tower receivers and global satellite tracking.

System Options

Engine Disabler/Kill Switch

This is an inexpensive option that can be used by itself, or as an add-on for an alarm system. Have an alarm company or auto electric shop install a hidden switch that will cut power to the starter. Simple and to the point - hot-wiring or using a key, if the starter can't spin, the thief can't win. I like that!

Bar Locking Device

These devices attach to the steering wheel and make driving the vehicle impossible. They also offer a high degree of protection from air-bag theft. Several companies make similar products. The "Club"™ is one you might recognize.

Armor Collar

A metal shield that wraps around your steering column, which prevents ignition tampering, and some types of "hot-wiring."

Wheel Locks

Common locking method for expensive rims and tires. The disadvantage associated with this product is the ease that the locking "tool" can be purchased. However, this is widely used as a deterrent that can stop or delay this type of theft.

Hood Lock

Makes engine parts difficult to steal and alarms difficult to disable.

Window Security Film

Window film is highly effective and makes breaking through the glass windows almost impossible. This product is used around the world for executive protection, but it is very expensive, but then again, cost is irrelevant, isn't it?

Fuel Switch

A simple and inexpensive device that stops the fuel-flow so the vehicle will only go a very short distance and then quits.

Time Delay Switch

This power cutoff mechanism, unless deactivated with a hidden switch, will disable your car shortly after starting. Usually the vehicle goes dead in about five hundred yards.

Time Delay Ignition

This nifty little widget will activate your ignition **only** after a preset time has passed. There is no way to activate the ignition before the preset time has elapsed. If your wife ever gets after you with a rolling pin, this might not be the system for you, although auto door locks and security film would help.

Clutch and Break Lock

If you have a manual transmission, this mechanism locks the break pedal and the clutch pedal together so one won't work without the other.

Alarm Systems/Components

- ✓ Keyless entry that allows you to open or lock the vehicle while arming or disarming the security alarm system.
- ✓ Electronic scan prevention stops the use of sophisticated electronic scanners that can decipher your system alarm code.
- ✓ Passive arming will allow your system to self-arm if the owner forgets to set the alarm.
- ✓ Built-in kill switch that will disable the ignition.
- ✓ Built-in fuel cut-off switch.
- ✓ Remote activated horn or siren.
- ✓ Glass-break sensor that sets off alarm when window is smashed.

- ✓ A proximity sensor that gives an audible voice warning if someone approaches within a pre-determined distance of the vehicle "Warning, Warning! Alarm! Step back! Alarm!"
- ✓ Hood/trunk sensor if someone tries to tamper with the hood or trunk.
- ✓ Remote pager that lets you know when an alarm is activated.
- ✓ Visible LED warning light that signals that an active alarm is protecting the vehicle.
- ✓ Remote starting device for cold weather or high security counter-measure for bomb threats.

Upscale system might include

- ✓ A high security coded and monitored starting transmitter system. When the vehicle is driven without first entering a special code the Alarm Company is alerted and can then track the vehicle. In the case of a carjacking, the owner can notify the Alarm Company and have the car shut off remotely.
- ✓ Remote door opening and vehicle starting for handicap drivers, Cold weather, arms full of packages, and high security counter measure.
- ✓ Global positioning pinpoints your location within a few feet, and gives you directional mapping for travel. Some programs, like OnStar, even keeps you in voice control with a monitoring station for directions, or emergencies, at the touch of a button.

I have attempted to give you a good overview of vehicle anti-theft devices, so you won't be as completely in the dark as I was. This represents only a fraction of this industry, but it was never my intent to write a book on vehicle anti-theft. With the information I have provided, you should be able to address your needs. Although most auto owners only want **Level #1 -** basic security, many others will require **Levels 2, 3, or 4.** The level of protection you select is directly tied to the value of your property, your lifestyle, and your budget. There are, of course, exceptions to every rule. There is always that consumer that simply wants all the whistles and bells he can afford. But for good crime management planning, I recommend you approach this issue with your needs in mind, and not your ego. When you start your search or upgrade for vehicle security, use this information as a starting point. Just by reading this book you will be considerably more informed than the average buyer, and information is power. I suggest you select three or four professional alarm companies, give them your basic requirements, and let them give you in-depth information for the level of protection that you want. By the time you get bids from three or four dealers, digest all you have learned, and make your choice, you will find it was time well spent. You select the best system for your needs while bidding your price, and because of researching and asking for detailed information; you will not wind up with buyer's remorse. Spend the time. It is a serious purchase. A well-planned decision cannot only save you money; it could also save your life.

A few last minute thoughts:

1. **Code hopping:** This is a term you may run across during your anti-theft search. Essentially, this is the term used when the alarm has the ability to change transmission codes each time the transmitter is activated. This prevents a thief from using a decoder to access your alarm's code. Most experts agree this is very difficult to do, seldom ever attempted, and the value is questionable. If the alarm has this feature, and the cost is reasonable, that is fine. However, do not let a silver tongued sales clerk tell you it is a "must have" piece of equipment.

2. **Duel Stage Sensor:** Pretty slick feature, but mostly for convenience. This is a two-stage alarm activation circuit that chirps if the vehicle is bumped, but activates the alarm if vibrations and shocks are repeated. Example; if I accidentally bump your vehicle with my car door…chirp, chirp! If I bump it a second time, it's show time!

3. **Passive Settings:** This was briefly mentioned before, but deserves more respect. Remember the states I mentioned that require insurance companies to give you a price break if your vehicle is equipped with an alarm? Passive Setting alarms are favored by insurance agencies, and often result in better rates because it cuts their claim risks. When you leave your car, it automatically sets the alarm. Of course insurance companies would like a feature like that, but so should you. All of us are guilty of forgetting once in awhile, but if we forget to activate the alarm, well, it could be a long and costly walk home. I recommend you consider this option.

STOLEN VEHICLE RECOVERY

Now that you have a better understanding of vehicle theft, and your vulnerability to this type of criminal action, let's discuss the various options we have to recover those missing vehicles before they find their way into the chop shops, or out of the country. Because of the tremendous cost involved in the auto theft industry, government, state, local law enforcement, insurance companies and the private sector have been scrambling to find a better mousetrap. Because this is a book on crime prevention and not criminal apprehension, I will not go into detail about recovery, but you should know some of the programs that are available.

Remember the two rules I mentioned earlier? Make a theft difficult to execute, and take the profit out of the crime. Now that's what I call crime management!

Vehicle Identification Number (VIN) Glass Etching

VIN numbers have been placed on vehicles since 1969. The VIN number can be found on a metal tag attached to the dash, near the window. It is also located somewhere on the body of the vehicle. Depending on the manufacturer, it could be on the engine, frame, transmission, etc.

When you report a vehicle theft, the VIN is sent to the National Crime Information Computer (NCIC) to aid in the recovery. As all law enforcement agencies are tied into this computerized network, it is a simple method to identify a stolen vehicle.

To enhance this VIN identification program, most states and local agencies now offer VIN GLASS ETCHING as a secondary theft deterrent. For example, in the State of Florida, the Florida Department of Motor Vehicles offers this program for free. The VIN is etched on all windows utilizing a chemical, or laser method, and when I had mine done it only took one minute to complete the process. Most authorities believe this is an excellent deterrent against professional thieves because this makes it necessary to replace all of the glass before selling the vehicle...a very costly, and time-consuming process. Contact your local police department for information about VIN "glass etching" in your area.

WATCH YOUR CAR PROGRAM (WYC)

WYC is commonly known as Watch Your Car Program. It is a project authorized under Title XXII of the Violent Crime Control and Law Enforcement Act of 1994 (42 U.S.C. 14171), which grants the Attorney General the power to develop, in cooperation with the states, a national voluntary **motor vehicle** theft prevention program.

The purpose of the WYC program is to identify potential stolen vehicles and enable law enforcement officers to conduct a preliminary check on an automobile <u>before</u> a stolen vehicle report is issued. This program is funded by a Federal program known as, Motor Vehicle Theft Prevention Act (MVTPA), and made available through grants for those states wishing to participate (Some states have a similar program of their own and do not use WYC). The funding allows those participating states to produce and distribute decals to resident vehicle owners that wish to safeguard their vehicles. When an automobile with the WYC decal is seen operating during early morning hours, or within the vicinity of international borders or ports, law enforcement officers have been given the owner's authorization to stop the vehicle, without

restrictions placed by probable cause constraints. By assessing information from either the state's Department of Motor Vehicle registration database, or an independent agency, an officer would be able to determine whether the operator of the vehicle should be further questioned, or detained for additional investigation for suspicion of vehicle theft, as provided in that jurisdiction.
You can find out more about this program by contacting the:
U.S. Department of Justice
Office of Justice Programs
Bureau of Justice Assistance
Washington, D.C.

All states have some form of stolen vehicle recovery, or interdiction program. If they are not using the national WYC program, most have developed a similar anti vehicle theft program. In Florida, the State Legislature, and the Florida Department of Law enforcement (FDLE) offers a voluntary program called Combat Auto Theft (CAT) that uses a very distinct Black Panther window decal. Residents of the participating counties register their vehicles with the Sheriff's Office. A CAT decal is then affixed to the inside front window of the driver's side, and to the inside rear window on the driver's side. As part of the registration agreement, displaying the decals allows law enforcement officers to conduct an investigative traffic stop, with no need for probable cause, between the hours of 1:00am and 5:00am to determine if the vehicle is stolen.
This program in no way restricts the registered owner from driving in those early morning hours, but simply gives police the flexibility to conduct early morning investigation stops before the vehicle is reported stolen. Statistics for the FBI Uniform Crime Report show that the majority of stolen vehicles occur during this early morning timeframe while your are still asleep, or at work. This is a very effective service, offered at no cost to the registered vehicle owners. Everyone should take advantage of this program, especially if you infrequently drive in these early morning hours.
Important: If you are registered with one of these programs, and you are stopped during those early morning hours, use

caution. **When the officer signals for you to pull over, consider using this procedure: Pull to the right side of the road, well out of the traffic flow, if possible. Turn on your four-way flashers, turn on your interior lights, roll the driver side window down, place both hands on the steering wheel, and wait for instructions from the officer. When those instructions are issued, comply exactly!**

When you sign up for one of these programs, there is an assumed understanding that you do not normally drive at these hours, and the officers will be using extreme caution in the event a simple investigative stop escalates into a felony stop. If you take this stop lightly, and play games with these officers, you could find yourself, unceremoniously, face down on the pavement with a very large bore semi-automatic firearm pointed at your head…Not where you want to be! Be courteous, remain calm, answer their questions, and you will be safely on your way after the officers verify that you are the registered owner of the vehicle. Remember, this is your program to safeguard your vehicle, and by your request. It is free, but it cannot work without some procedural guidelines. This is for your protection, as well as the officers. By the way, check with your insurance company to see if you qualify for a premium discount rate.

For more information on the CAT program, contact your local sheriff's office.

Because auto theft is so pervasive in the United States, industry watchers are predicting almost two million vehicles will be stolen in the year 2001. It is little wonder that vehicle owners are scrambling for anti-theft devices, and recovery programs. One program I like is the **LoJack Stolen Vehicle Recovery System.** LoJack works in cooperation with police, nationwide, A LoJack transmitter is randomly hidden in your vehicle by a LoJack technician. If your vehicle is stolen, you report the theft to the police, who then activates the LoJack Recovery System over a police telecommunication network. Once activated, the hidden transmitter in your vehicle starts transmitting a silent coded signal, allowing a specially equipped police vehicle to use a tracking computer to recover the vehicle. Whether moving or stopped, the tracking computer tells the police where the target vehicle is, and leads them to it. Four rooftop antennas on the vehicle roof identify a police unit with a LoJack tracking device. Once the unit locks onto the stolen vehicle, there is a 90% recovery rate, and for that reason, check with your insurance carrier for a reduction on your rates.

The LoJack warranty is impressive. If your LoJack equipped vehicle is stolen within the two-year period and not recovered by the police within 24 hours of your stolen vehicle report, your LoJack Retrieve System purchase price will be refunded. I like what that says about this system! Actually there are five different LoJack systems to satisfy the level of protection you require.

System I
Basic LoJack Retrieval System
System II
LoJack Retrieval and Starter Disabler
System III
LoJack Retrieval, Starter Disabler, and Alert Alarm
System IV
LoJack Retrieval, Starter Disabler, Alert Alarm and Keyless Entry
System V
LoJack Retrieval, Starter Disabler, Alert Alarm for vehicles with factory keyless entry
All Systems Include:
- **Installation**
- **No Monthly Fees**
- **Permanent Installation on the Vehicle**

For additional information, check with your local sheriff's office, your car dealer, or Auto Nation's Financial Services, or you may contact LoJack at the following:
LoJack Corporation
Corporate Headquarters

333 Elm Street
Dedham, MA 02026
www.lojack.com

Traveling the roads and highways of America can be a wonderful experience. This is truly a beautiful country, and the vast majority of people you meet are good, honest people. Unfortunately, auto travel can also be dangerous. Forewarned is forearmed. I hope the information in the Auto/Travel section of this book will help keep you and your loved ones from harm's way. I urge you to look for other publications of this nature, take advantage of personal safety classes in your area, and use the information in this book to establish a personal safety strategy for every member of your family. Doing so will give you a distinct advantage if you come face to face with crime and violence. Most criminal encounters are spontaneous and poorly planned, and can be easily defeated with good crime prevention training.

Nothing gives one person so much advantage over another as to remain cool and unruffled under all circumstances.
THOMAS JEFFERSON (1743-1826)

SUGGESTED READING:

➤ **The Gift of Fear**, by Gavin Be Becker. Dell publishing

➤ **How To Protect Yourself from Crime**, by Ira A. Lipman. Reader's Digest

➤ **The Seven Steps To Personal Safety**, by Tim Powers & Richard B. Isaacs, M.A. Published By: Center for Personal Defense Studies

CHAPTER FIVE

Home Security

"The world is a dangerous place to live, not because of the people who are evil, but because of the people who don't do anything about it." – Albert Einstein

While the first part of Hard Target addressed auto and travel safety issues, this section will focus on home security. I have already talked at some length on the dramatic decrease in crime, in almost every category, over the last five years. Latest figures out are suggesting as much as ten to fifteen percent reductions in almost all of the crime indexes and the leading experts in crime prevention are quick to hold this up as a banner of achievement. Well, we are making inroads. Massive amounts of money, time, and a national commitment to manage the crime problems have indeed reduced the overall volume. However, when you consider that America is the most crime ridden and violent country in the free world, the euphoria fades in the harsh light of reality, and the statistics simply mean that we had far too much crime in the first place. We are not even close to winning this war, only a few skirmishes. Crime and violence is alive and well, and like death and taxes, it's not going away in the near future. Am I a pessimist? No! I just don't want you to adopt a complacent attitude that will cloud your judgment and make you a victim.

When evaluating your home security needs, the first thing to remember is that no house is "Burglar Proof." If he wants in, he is coming in. With that in mind, your goal should be to make yourself a "Hard Target." Make yourself less desirable to the thief and he will find another suitor. He will simply look elsewhere. Will securing your home stop crime and violence? No! It only diverts it from your home to another. Whenever a thief is out prowling for a victim, it is safe to say he will be able to satisfy his craving, just don't allow yourself to be on his menu. Your primary goal is to protect your immediate family and loved ones. Unfortunately, the burglar does not have to go very far to find "Welcome Burglar" signs that signal an easy target. Let's make a concerted effort to make our homes less desirable to thieves and safer for ourselves. If you want to do something to help keep your friends from harm's way, share this book with your next-door neighbor, and have them pass it on. As crime prevention information gathers momentum within a community, it provides the essential building blocks necessary for a safer environment for everyone (except the thief).

Home security is an issue that needs to be taken seriously. If you allow the crime reduction figures to lull you into a self-contented posture, you are then allowing yourself and your family members to become easy targets for the criminal. In the back of your mind, where reason and common sense reside, you know that good security and avoidance is the best course of action, yet many citizens still resist. It would be wonderful if crime and violence could be wiped out completely and maybe some day it will be, but until that day comes, walk softly and carry a big stick.

STARTING YOUR PLAN

Before you rush to the hardware store and begin buying various tool and products to create a safe haven for you and your loved ones, you must first consider the facility you are going to harden (make more secure). Do you own the property, or are you a renter? If you are the owner, head for the hardware store without delay. On the other hand, if you rent a house or apartment, own a condominium or live in a deed restricted community, or gated complex, you need to discuss your security concerns with the actual owner, homeowner's association, or security personnel before making any changes to the property, or security company. In the case of renting, once you add anything to a property it could be considered a "property of the owner," and if you should relocate, those improvements cannot be removed. Also, in a deed-restricted community many restrictions might apply regarding lighting, burglar bars, alarms, or dogs.

Yes, you absolutely have the right to protect yourself, but in this time and age you are well advised to be sensitive to any property rights in your rental agreement or homeowner's covenants. It would sure be sad if you were charged with violating a tenant agreement, when all you are trying to do is protect yourself from being victimized. I recommend you talk first with your neighborhood watch group leader, or the homeowner's association. In the case of apartment rentals, definitely bring your concerns to the manager or property Management Company responsible. They will often make changes at their expense when an issue of personal tenant security is viewed as a liability. In addition, always, contact your local law enforcement agencies for advice. They welcome a proactive approach from the community, and realize that the better informed you are, the less crime and violence they have to deal with. Most departments have excellent crime prevention programs designed for your specific needs and lifestyle. Don't forget, they are also your friends and neighbors, and they have the same concerns that most of us have ...protecting ourselves, friends and loved ones from crime and violence.

My dad used to tell me, "Joe, if you're going to do something, put your brain in gear before you tell your feet to move."

Protecting ourselves from crime and violence is not difficult, it just requires some good information that helps us make better decisions. Ready, Fire, Aim, does not work real well.

Beware of "lock" thieves:

Let us play a little what-if game, and find out if you are ready to throw caution to the wind, and believe crime will not happen to you…only the other person! Just say, for the sake of this little exercise, that you and your family go out for a Saturday morning breakfast, and leave your house unattended. While you are enjoying your meal, I make an uninvited visit to your home, and I remove all of your locks. All I steal is the locks. I carry a big bag and I take all the locks out of every door in your house, and put them in my big burglar bag. I then take all of the locks from the windows, and I put these in my bag. I take the locks from the garage door, the storage shed, and even take the locks off the gate. I steal every lock in your home, whistling while I work, and then I leave with my burglar bag stuffed full of all your locks. When you arrive home, feeling full and contented after a pleasant morning out with your loved ones, you are speechless when you realize that someone has stolen all the locks from your house. As you and the family frantically run throughout the house, you discover that every lock is gone, and only the holes remain as grim evidence that you have become a victim. Your poor wife is in a state of fearful shock to suddenly realize that her safe haven has been violated. The kids are in a panic when they also realize that even the locks on their bedroom doors are missing. You slowly recover your composure, as anger and frustration flood your mind with mixed emotions. After you call the police, all of the reports have been finished, and you are standing dumbfounded in your lockless house, what do you do? It is obvious you will have to replace the locks. When will you do that? Will you replace them tomorrow, next week, wait until payday, or will you replace them before you and your family goes to bed that evening? My guess is you would not let any moss grow under your feet getting down to the local hardware to buy new locks.

Why would you want to replace them before you go to bed that evening? Because you think, an intruder might sneak into your house sometime in the future? No! You would replace those locks immediately because to do otherwise would place your entire family in a vulnerable position. You would be in harm's way

Chapter Five   Home Security

should the lock thief return, or some other thief realizes you had no perimeter protection. In other words, you would be fearful that you and your family could become victims of crime and violence that very evening. I hope this little exercise breaks any apathy barriers, and it helps you to clearly understand that crime does not only happen to the other guy…remember, to the other guy, you are the other guy.
Just because you live in a nice, quiet neighborhood does not give you immunity from crime. To make my point indelible, have you ever seen a lake when the water was as smooth as glass, and everything was calm and peaceful? That does not necessarily mean there is not an alligator in the water. Whenever I sit on my patio, on a quiet summer evening, I can't help wondering if there is an alligator, out there in the dark, quietly looking for an opportunity.

Now that I have your attention, and you understand your vulnerability, it is time to introduce you to some options that will dramatically reduce your chances of becoming a victim.

FBI CRIME REPORT STATISTICS

- ❖ Every 13 seconds a home is burglarized.
- ❖ Over 2.5 million burglaries per year.
- ❖ 8,600 break-ins every day.
- ❖ 85% of all break-ins are through a doorway.
- ❖ 66% of all burglars are forced entries.
- ❖ 1 out of 3 residential assaults are a result of a burglary.
- ❖ 51% of break-ins occur during daylight.
- ❖ 49% of break-ins occur after dark.
- ❖ 85% of break-ins are committed by non-professionals/often desperate and dangerous.

NOTE: These statistics may very slightly, depending on research data, and the timeframe that the study was conducted. Every attempt has been made to provide up to date information and statistics throughout this book, and should only vary slightly by publication date. However, many statistical databanks, and demographic reports are only analyzed every three to five years. While I have practiced due-diligence in writing this book, some of the data will appear somewhat dated. If you want more updated information, I encourage you to use the resources found in Hard Copy, to advance your understanding of crime and violence, and provide options to keep you and your loved ones safe in the troubled times to come.

SECURITY BEGINS WITH A STATE OF MIND!
Statistics like these are commonly found in the newspapers, magazines, and television, and although they may vary slightly, they generally portray an accurate picture of our vulnerability to crime and violence. Crime and violence in America is a popular topic for writers and readers alike. Unfortunately, until you become the victim, most treat this subject like a television series; we tune in, from time to time, just to catch the excitement, and then switch back to our favorite program. The longer we survive "Crime–Free," the more complacent we become. Some will go years before being touched by crime, but rarely does anyone go from the cradle to the grave without becoming a victim. I personally have never met a person over the age of 40 that has not had an experience with crime, violence, or both, by one degree or another.

- More than four out of five Americans (85%) are personally "very concerned" about violent crime...**National Center for Crime Victims.**

- 54% of Americans report that violent crime is more of a problem in their communities now than it was ten years ago...**National Victims Center.**

- One out of nine citizens are active, to some degree, in a community crime prevention group. That translates to more than 27 million Americans...**National Crime Prevention Council.**

If we are to believe the statistics, and the evidence is overwhelming, it is time for individuals, businesses, and the communities in general to increase their efforts toward crime prevention. As I mentioned earlier, recent data indicates that crime and violence is dropping in almost every category. Let us keep that trend going, but on the other hand, do not kid yourself. In 2001, the State of Florida had over 900,000 felony crimes, and that is just one state. Trust me, even when we see crime rates dropping, there is plenty to go around for everyone. You do not have to feel left out, but you should want to.

RESIDENTIAL BURGLARY

Residential burglary is commonplace throughout America because it is easy. One element of this crime is a need for money, the other element is a supply of goods that can be converted to money. Supply and demand; necessary ingredients for any financial venture. There are many motivational factors that cause a person to burglarize our homes, but the leading reason is drugs. With the proliferation of drugs, and the sub-culture that many users live in, various narcotics are in demand because they are addictive. They are also very expensive. Most addicts, and even casual users, spend a great deal of their time and energy in the acquisition of drugs, and spend thousands of dollars in the process. To take care of this supply and demand problem, burglary is the crime of choice for many addicts. Generally considered non-violent, easy to do, difficult to catch, and sentencing is light if they are caught. The money is good, and many homeowners seem to encourage the crime by leaving their homes unlocked and well stocked with valuables. Maintain a good inventory on your valuables. Record serial numbers on items like stereos, televisions, and other electronics. Keep a picture gallery of valuables. One good way to register your property is by room. Address each room, one at a time, and do a photo layout. Date the photos, and remember to upgrade photos on a regular basis. Secure the list of model and identification numbers and the photos, in a safe deposit box. This will be invaluable for crime identification and recovery, but also extremely helpful for insurance claims.

THE #1 PREVENTIVE MEASURE FOR BURGLARY AND HOME INTRUSION ARE SECURE DOORS.

The best crime prevention experts, including the FBI, National Sheriff's Association, National Victim Center, and the National Crime Prevention Council, and others, all agree that secure doors offer the greatest deterrent value to keep you from becoming a victim. The general consensus indicates between a 78 to 85 percent loss reduction when a home has intrusion resistant doors and windows. Simply put, you are 78 to 85 percent less likely to become a victim if you have proper door and window security in the home—that is significant!

Although it is almost impossible to build a totally secure house, you can make a dwelling very difficult, and time consuming for an intruder. National statistics from the FBI Uniform Crime Report shows that a burglar will spend no more than two minutes, on average, attempting illegal entry. They want what you have, and have no qualms about taking it, but they do not want to be caught. If they cannot gain quick access without being detected, they just go look for another house that is easier.

HOW A THIEF GAINS ACCESS THROUGH DOORS

1. **He knocks on the door and if nobody answers,** he tries the door. If it is unlocked (30% are) he simply walks in.
2. **He knocks on the door, and if nobody answers**, he simply kicks the door in. Most door striker plates are secured with 2 tiny screws that give quickly to a forceful kick by an intruder. They can usually get in quicker than you can with a key.
3. **He knocks on the door, if nobody answers;** he uses a lock pick set to open the door. Most burglars and home intruders are amateur in nature, and these devices are seldom used. The professional burglar will use pick sets, bypass burglar alarms,

and implement detailed planning, but only if the dwelling has something of great value known to the perpetrator.
4. **He knocks on the door, and if no one answers...**
   A. He will act like he's lost, and ask for directions, and leave, or;
   B. He will take advantage of the opportunity, force his way in, and now the simple plan for an unoccupied burglary of a dwelling, becomes a violent home invasion.

KEEP A LOCKED DOOR POLICY. DO NOT OPEN YOUR DOORS TO STRANGERS. SECURE YOUR DOORS TO MAKE UNLAWFUL ENTRY DIFFICULT. DOORS

<u>**ENTRY DOORS**</u>: The best security is a **steel door**, with re-enforced striker plates and modified hinges. However, a steel door does not have to be unattractive. Doors today retrofitted with a wide variety of very attractive trim appliqués, that when painted, look like a custom finished wooden door.

A **solid, hardwood door**, mounted with re-enforced striker plates, can also provide a very good deterrent value. Use striker plates with 4 to 6 screws, a minimum of one inch in length.

1. ALL DOORS SHOULD HAVE A GOOD QUALITY DEADBOLT LOCK THAT EXTENDS, AT A MINIMUM, ONE INCH INTO THE DOORFRAME.
2. DOORS WITH GLASS SHOULD USE A DOUBLE DEADBOLT LOCK (KEY LOCKS FROM BOTH SIDES).
3. ALL SOLID DOORS SHOULD HAVE A WIDE ANGLE PEEPHOLE.
4. DOOR HINGEPINS SHOULD BE ON THE INSIDE.
5. DOORS WITH OUTSIDE HINGE PINS SHOULD BE "PIN-SECURED" (more about this later).

6. NEVER USE HOLLOW CORE DOORS FOR EXTERIOR DOOR SECURITY, INCLUDING A HOUSE ENTRY DOOR FROM THE GARAGE.

Glass front doors obviously present a security problem. Glass, after all, is a breakable substance that even a rank amateur thief can break with little effort. However, statistics indicate that breaking the glass on a door is not the entry of preference. Remember the mind of the average thief. He does not want to be caught. Noise attracts attention. A smashed front glass door is a red flag to a neighbor, or passing motorist. He will, however, break a glass panel to get at the thumb-switch of a deadbolt lock. Stylish leaded glass sections are the easiest to break out.

Use double deadbolt locks on doors with glass, or entryways with glass side panels next to doors.

You may want to check the existing fire codes in your area. Because of fire hazards, in rare cases, doors are not allowed to have key-locking deadbolts on the inside, only thumb release mechanisms.

PEEPHOLES: A good wide-angle door viewer is necessary for good crime prevention. You should use these devices in all solid doors. Do not forget the garage access door. I know you will never leave the garage door open, but just in case you do, a peephole allows you to look before opening the door. One rather clever one is called Door Scope, now becoming widely popular. This simple to install device allows you a wide-angle view from up to six feet from the door. It is almost impossible to open the door to an unwanted visitor. One distinct advantage of the Door Scope, a short child or wheel bound person can also easily view anyone outside your door. Disadvantage…you need extra good lighting on the other side of the door. That said, I have Door Scopes in all exterior doors of my home.

DOOR FRAMES: While steel doorframes are the most secure, few residential facilities are built with "good" security in mind. **Aluminum framing** is a poor second, and easy to circumvent. **Solid hardwood** offers formidable resistance to forced entry if equipped with proper hardware. Normal residential framing material is **fur or pine**, but once again, using appropriate security hardware and quality locks can make illegal entry both time-consuming and difficult.

THE STRONGEST DOOR OFFERS MINIMUM PROTECTION WHEN INSTALLED IN A WEAK FRAME AND BASIC HARDWARE. **DO NOT BE PENNY WISE AND POUND FOOLISH.**

SECURITY CHAINS: A very poor defense for home invasion. This fixture is easy to force open with minimum effort. If you are going to install a chain, use long screws, and short prayers. Please forgive me if I sound flip on this subject. One limited advantage of chain locks is to serve notice that the dwelling might be occupied, causing someone with criminal intent to leave. On the other hand, once in a dwelling they can provide some delay for a thief if the homeowner comes home during the robbery.

Most security experts only favor chain devices if they are high tensile strength steel, secure with three inch screws firmly attached to a hardwood or metal framework. I favor a simple rubber wedge that will allow a person to open the door slightly, while holding your foot on the wedge. If someone tries to force the door open, this can be very effective. However, this conversation leads right backs to my favorite defense; don't open the door unless you know it is safe. Not a real difficult plan to put into your arsenal of strategic defenses.

SLIDING GLASS DOORS

With the huge popularity and demand for sliding glass doors, manufacturers are aware of the venerability and security of their product, but their dominant focus is on esthetic and energy efficient improvement to the home. This is not to downplay innovative engineering advances that have addressed the issue of security. However, it has been largely played down, with the exception of the builder or homeowner that is building or buying with security as a priority.

Why? Let us address that question straight on. If you had a manufacturing facility, or a retail showroom, and sliding doors that retails for...let's pick a number...$2,000.00, would you put your sales effort toward beautiful and efficient, or would you discuss the ease of which the average sliding door can be breached? Trust me, they do not even want the subject of security to come up. Of course, they mention deadbolt or integrated pin locking functions, they talk about the quality of the lock design, and the ease of operation, but they never talk about the venerability of their products. Simply put, they are trying to make a sale.

How does a thief get past a sliding glass door? Well, some might just break the glass and walk right into your house, however, that is unlikely for a number of reasons.
1. Shattering a glass door is a good way to alert the neighbors to an unwanted intruder.
2. The popularity of new thermal pane plastics makes breaking very difficult.
3. Advanced window film technology makes breaking all but impossible.
4. Burglars want "quick & easy," or look for a new target that meets their needs.

For most sliding doors, entry is a piece of cake. They simply slip a small curved pry-bar under the bottom of the door, step down on the bar, and lift the door out of the track. Quick and easy. Sliding doors are designed to lift out of the track for easy repair or replacement. Bad guys know this. They might not be able to spell *sliding door*, but they know how they function, and they can spot the easy ones and can lift them out of the track about as quick as a homeowner can open one with a key. They do this in a very quiet and efficient manner, thus allowing them an opening large enough for a big screen television, or anything else they want to take. A $5.95 tool, readily available at the local hardware store, and they are in your home. I might add, that simple pry-bar can be a formidable weapon when the homeowner suddenly confronts them. As I have said before, there is only one thing worse than a burglary when you are **not** home and that is one when you **are** home. If you suddenly encounter a burglary in progress, things can get ugly in a heartbeat. Especially if you come face to face with a desperate thief with a steel pry-bar in his hand.

Is there a solution? Yes, if you must have sliding doors, make sure the security aspects of the door you choose are equal or better than the esthetic value. Is a high security sliding door expensive? Yes! But to ignore security can have a deadly cost.

Having said all this, I can suggest a security measure that will cost you less than a dollar, and requires only a few minutes to implement. This will not work in all cases, but it will secure most doors from being lifted out of the framework. Go to your local hardware store and buy four "Tapcon" self-tapping screws. These are usually blue in color. Open each sliding door, and drill a starter hole in the upper door channel of each door, about 18 inches apart. Set the screws until they just barely clear the door in its track. Now when someone tries to pry the door out of the track, the top of the door will hit the screw head, and it will not have enough clearance to allow it to be lifted out of the track. A simple and cost effective alternative to becoming a victim. By thinking outside the box, you have just adopted another component to your personal safety strategy, and you are putting the odds in your favor. You are making yourself a hard target.

I have taken some time on the issue of sliding doors, only because they are a popular point of entry in most dwellings. If your doors are not secure, if you fail to address this security weak point, I have failed with the intent of this book…but you could be the biggest loser.

The fear of burglars is not only the fear of being robbed, but also the fear of a sudden and unexpected clutch out of the

darkness. — **Elias Canetti (1905 – 94), Author: "The Fear of Being Touched."**
With residential burglary increasing at an alarming rate, experts are scrambling for answers. It is certainly not uncommon to find a law enforcement conference room crowed with sociologists, psychologists, psychiatrists, homebuilders, and social workers. At that same table, you should not be surprised to fire alarm company representatives, security consultants, manufacturers, representatives, and citizen patrol members. A collective effort and a cross section of people from all lifestyles, taking a proactive approach to the problems of crime and violence that concern all of us. Nevertheless, there is no magic bullet. A crime is a very complex by-product of American society, and constantly in a process of flux and changes that makes crime management challenging. We are not winning the war, but we are developing strategic options to address cause and effect, thus providing the foundation for avoidance, prevention, and apprehension and convection, of those that would make crime targets of innocent citizens.
HOW DO YOU STOP A BURGLAR? **YOU CANNOT!** You can only make it difficult for him to practice his profession on you and your family, and hope your security efforts will discourage him enough that he will go away. When he leaves, will he target some other family? Probably, but that is not your fault, nor is that your immediate concern.

DO NOT BECOME COMPLACENT OR OVER CONFIDENT, EVEN THOUGH YOU PRACTICE A LOCKED DOOR POLICY.
I am reminded of the person that told me he could not be robbed because he ALWAYS keeps his doors and windows locked.

Always! I asked if he had ever locked himself out of his house. He answered, "Yes." I then asked if he ever got back in…

Food for thought: Crime statistics throughout this book only reflect those crimes that were REPORTED.

Chapter Five   Home Security

The following home security checklist is important. Give it the time it deserves. Although we realize that we can never make our homes "Burglar Proof," we can do many things that will discourage the criminals by practicing good crime management deterrents.

The following checklist is for *your* protection. I've already completed mine. Addressing these issues will not guarantee your safety, but it will significantly reduce your risk of becoming a victim. Each "NO" indicates a breach of security that you have overlooked. When you are made aware of a potentially dangerous situation, fix it. Your life could depend on it.

Part of this checklist pertains to your house when you are gone. The biggest mistake you can make is to think that a crime committed while you are away is not a direct personal threat. The only thing worse than a property crime when you are away, is one when you are there. If you come home and are confronted by an intruder in your home, a simple act of burglary of an unoccupied dwelling can quickly escalate into a much more dangerous situation. Carefully consider each of these questions, take them serious, and continue the process of removing yourself as an easy target.

There are literally mountains of crime prevention programs available, in even the smallest communities in America, and I encourage you to contact your local law enforcement agency to see what is available in your specific area. One program that stands out from my research is Contra Costa County Sheriff's Office in California. Under the leadership of Sheriff Warren E. Ruff, I consider their crime prevention programs among the top 10. For example, in 2001, the California Crime Prevention Officer's Association selected Contra Costa Sheriff's Office as the winner of the Crime Prevention Program of the Year for their Community Oriented Policing program, I.C.O.P. Sheriff Ruff has been with the department for over 35 years, and continues to this day to improve the security and well being of the citizens under his charge.

Chapter Five   Home Security

With permission, I am enclosing the "Check List" from their web site, http://www.cocosheriff.org/homesecurity.
Remember that this checklist only points out your weak areas. The more questions you answer with "yes" will determine your level of security. It may seem that I am repeating myself from previous content, but this is meant to be interactive…get your pencil! Do it now! As in every aspect of security, attitude, frame of mind and a proactive individual commitment to these issues can improve your quality of life.

CHECK LIST

SAFE PRACTICES AND OPERATION I.D.

1. Do you belong to a Neighborhood Watch Program? Yes__ No__
2. Do you keep a list of all valuable property? Yes___ No___
3. Do you have a list of the serial numbers of your electronic equipment? Yes___ No___
4. Do you have a description of other property that does not have a serial number? Yes___ No___
5. Have you taken videotapes of your jewelry, antiques, or collectibles? Yes___ No___
6. Do you avoid unnecessary display or publicity of your valuables? Yes___ No___
7. Do you keep excess cash and other valuables in the bank? Yes___ No___
8. Do you plan so that you do not need to hide a key on your property? Yes___ No___
9. Have you told your family what to do if they discover a burglar breaking in or already in the house? Yes___ No___
10. Have you told your family to leave the house undisturbed and call the sheriff if they discover a burglary has been committed? Yes___ No___

11. Do you have emergency phone numbers listed by your phone? Yes___ No___
12. Do you know the non-emergency number for the police or sheriff's office? Yes___ No___
13. Is your house number illuminated and easily visible from the street during all hours? Yes___ No___
14. Have you locked up your ladder and avoided trellises or drainpipes that could be used by a burglar to climb to the second floor or roof? Yes___ No___
15. Are lights installed around the perimeter of your house? Yes___ No___
16. Is the front door well lit? Yes___ No___
17. Is the back door well lit? Yes___ No___
18. Are exterior lights controlled by photocell? Yes___ No___
19. Is public or residence lighting sufficient to illuminate all sides of the dwelling? Yes___ No___
20. Are shrubs and bushes trimmed to a maximum height of 42 inches? Yes___ No___
21. Are large trees trimmed so the lower branches are more than seven (7) feet off the ground? Yes___ No___
22. Are trees and bushes trimmed to eliminate hiding places? Yes___ No___
23. Are ground plants under windows maintained at a height that is below the windowsill? Yes___ No___
24. Are your exterior doors of solid core construction? Yes___ No___
25. Do entry doors have a wide-angle optical viewer? Yes___ No___
26. Do exterior doors have cylinder-type deadbolt locks with at least a one inch throw and beveled cylinder guard? Yes___ No___
27. Do the doors without cylinder locks have a heavy bolt or some similar secure device that can be operated only from the inside? Yes___ No___
28. Can all your doors (Basement, Porch, French, Balcony and Garage) be securely locked? Yes___ No___

29. Are your locks in good repair? Yes___ No___
30. Are the door strike plates (the jam fastening that receives the bolt in the locking position) installed with three (3) inch screws? Yes___ No___
31. Do you know anyone that has a key to your house? Or are keys still in position of previous owners and friends? Yes___ No___
32. Do all out-swinging doors have a hinge with a locking pin or non-removable pins? Yes___ No___
33. Are entry areas unobstructed by shrubbery and other décor to permit maximum visibility? Yes___ No___
34. Does the porch light have a minimum 60-watt bulb? Yes___ No___
35. Do the sliding doors have an auxiliary lock that locks both the door panels together or active side to the frame? Yes___ No___
36. Is the garage door secured with a padlock, hasp, or other good auxiliary lock? Do you use it? Yes___ No___
37. Is your interior door from the garage to your home treated as an exterior door in terms of security? (Solid core, deadbolt, etc.) Yes___ No___
38. Do you lock your car and take the keys out even when it is locked in your garage? Yes___ No___
39. Do you lock your garage doors whenever you are not in the garage? Yes___ No___
40. Do you leave the garage door opener in a visible spot in your car? Yes___ No___
41. Do you remove all valuables from plain sight in your vehicle? Yes___ No___

WINDOWS

42. Are all windows equipped with auxiliary locks or pinned? Yes___ No___
43 Have you replaced or secured louvered windows? Yes___ No___
44. Are your window locks properly and securely mounted? Yes___ No___

Chapter Five   Home Security

45. Do you keep your windows locked when they are shut? Yes___ No___
46. Do you have good, secure locks on garage windows? Yes___ No___
47. Do you have garage windows covered with curtains or blinds? Yes___ No___
48. Are you as careful of basement and second floor windows as you are of those on the first floor? Yes___ No___
49. Do you have defensive plants (large thorny plants) planted below easily accessible windows? Yes___ No___
50. Have you removed items below windows that could be used to reach the window? Yes___ No___
51. Do you keep your drapes drawn at night so people can't see in your home? Yes___ No___
52. Can windows left open for ventilation be secured? Yes___ No___

VACATION

53. Did you stop all deliveries and arrange for a trusted neighbor or family member to pick up your mail, newspapers and packages? Yes___ No___
54. Did you ask a trusted neighbor to watch your residence while you are away? Yes___ No___
55. Did you leave your vacation address and telephone number with a trusted neighbor so you can be reached in case of an emergency? Yes___ No___
56. Did you test your smoke and burglar alarm? Yes___ No___
57. Did you arrange for someone to mow your yard, rake leaves and maintain the yard to give the home a lived in look? Yes___ No___
58. Did you plug in timers to turn lights, radio and television on and off at appropriate times? Yes___ No___
59. Did you turn the bell or ringer on the telephones down low, or off? Yes___ No___
60. If you have call forwarding, did you have your calls forwarded to a trusted friend or relative? Yes___ No___

61. Did you leave shades and blinds in a normal position?
    Yes___ No___
62. Did you close and lock garage doors and windows?
    Yes___ No___
63. Did you ask a neighbor to park in your driveway so it appears someone is home? Yes___ No___
64. Did you ask the police or sheriff's office for a vacation house check while you are away? Yes___ No___

Now that you have checked yes or no, total the yes's and the no's, and if you have more no's checked, it's time to get busy! You do not have to be an expert or invest a lot of money to improve the security of your home, but security should be appropriate to the value you place on your property and family. To invest in a home (for most of us, the single biggest investment) and not provide adequate security is like wearing a tuxedo with tennis shoes...dumb!

RECAP

- Crime is down in almost every category...Riiiight!
- Do not let a complacent attitude cloud your mind.
- Develop a hard target attitude.
- Walk softly, and carry a big stick.
- Do not believe crime only happens to the other guy.
- Beware of the lock thief.
- Replace missing or inadequate locks promptly.
- 1 out of every 3 home assaults result from a burglary.
- Every 13 seconds a home is burglarized.
- Get involved in crime prevention.
- Record serial numbers on valuables.
- Photo layout of rooms for insurance.
- Use safety deposit box.
- #1 preventative measure...locked doors and windows deny quick access.
- Thieves have a plan...do you?
- A knock on the door should make you cautious.

Chapter Five — Home Security

- Don't open doors to strangers.
- Do you have a peephole?
- Solid doors bring solid results.
- Double deadbolt where warranted.
- Strong doors, weak hardware, bad news.
- Security chains provide a good laugh.
- We have a long way to go before the war is won.
- Tapcon's are not a bad idea for sliding doors.
- Security begins with a change of attitude.

The National Center for Crime Victims report that 4 out of 5 citizens are concerned about crime…Are you concerned enough to make yourself a Hard Target? I place enormous value on understanding the other person. A casual friendship, a business venture, or someone intent on harming me physically or financially. Understanding your adversary transfers power of logical thinking, and logical thinking is the best of all body armors.

CHAPTER SIX

Gangs

While the main objective of Hard Target is meant to be a starting point that helps you develop personal safety strategies, it is also a wakeup call for many. By its very nature, crime and violence is distasteful, and a subject most keep locked in a secure never-never land of their minds. "This will never-never happen to me." But in the harsh reality of the real world, all of us brush elbows with danger on a daily basis, we just don't see it, or have a tendency to close our eyes and wait for it to go away when it does rear its ugly head. Most bystanders do not want to get involved thinking they are ill equipped to handle it, and besides, crime is not their problem. I call this the "Ostrich Syndrome." It is easier to stick our heads in the sand when we fail to understand something, thereby blocking the crime from view until the danger passes…or leave it for someone else to resolve.

Once a person stops giving lip service to the problems of crime and violence, and adopts a proactive approach to the issues, then, and only then, can that person begin the process required to protect themselves and their loved ones. It is not difficult; it just takes planning with your eyes wide open. We begin by accepting the fact that crime and violence *can* touch us at some time in our lives, and it does not just happen to someone other than ourselves. That is easy. Think about this; if crime did not exist, law enforcement agencies would not exist. Now that you firmly accept the basic fact that crime is a part of our world, we can continue to examine the problem, and review the best options for any given situation we encounter.

As we look at the problem of gang violence, do not let yourself slip into the safe belief that you are far removed from this behavior. Many citizens, communities and institutions have a tendency to deny gang problems for political, economic and perceptual reasons. Public denial of the existence of gangs or the seriousness of the problem, coupled with a lack of proactive community measures are major contributing factors to the alarming increase in the number, size, and strength of gangs. Gang violence is a stark reality, rapidly growing, and very dangerous...and your community is not exempt, regardless where you live in America.

The United States Office of Juvenile Justice and Delinquency estimated 26,000 gangs in 1999 (this is juvenile, not adult organizations).
According to the National Youth Gang Surveys, gang membership has grown from 55,000 members in 1975, to over 900,000 gang members' ln 1999.

The National Institute of Justice estimates that the financial costs of violent gang crime to American society is well over $450 billion a year.

The issue of gang crime is much more than financial costs to the American taxpayer. Youth gangs directly threatens the quality of life in our communities, and are effectively taking our youth hostage by offering a false sense of pride, loyalty, and trust, that many parents have failed to provide. If we fail to instill values such as love, appreciation, family structure, rules and consequences, and we fail to lead our children by example, they will look for basic needs outside the family. This is only one dad's opinion, and I am not trying to impose my standards of parenting on my readers, but the issues are too important to brush over lightly. Secondly, without providing an overview to the problem, it makes finding safeguard solutions significantly more difficult. If you should find yourself confronted by a gang member, how could you choose the best course of action unless you know what's in his head?

To understand the motivations that lead our youth into a world of gang activity and crime is much too complicated to explain in a chapter, and that is not what this book is trying to do. If you have teenage children and feel uncomfortable with their behavior, or have friends that need help, get involved. There are many excellent books of anti-social adolescent behavior, and child psychology that can be invaluable when looking for answers you are untrained and poorly equipped to deal with. Children are well worth this effort, and it does take effort, but those efforts could save a life. There are many social outreach organizations, school counselors, and church programs are well prepared to help families sort through difficult problems before they get to the crisis point, and even afterwards. Make that extra effort to reach beyond your frustration, and don't let go.

In her book, Lisbeth Schorr's **_Within Our Reach_** outlines four causative factors that are worth repeating. By no stretch of the imagination should one think these are the only reasons we lose our children, but they do point out some primary causes that you should explore in more depth if you know a child in distress, or send signals that say "Help me!"

Poverty: A sense of hopelessness can result from being able to purchasing certain goods and services. Young people living in poverty may find it difficult to meet basic physical and psychological needs which can lead to lack of self worth and pride, no matter how misplaced. Gang activity and crime provide the money to fill these needs.

Racism: When young people encounter both personal and institutional racism, their risks are often increased. When certain individuals and groups are denied power, privileges, and resources, they will often form their own anti-establishment group (i.e., street gangs).

Lack of Support Network: Gang members often come from homes where they feel alienated or neglected. They may then turn to gangs when these basic needs of love and understanding are not met at home. These risks increase substantially when the community fails to provide well-organized youth programs and facilities that contribute to, and recognize achievement and value from meaningful efforts.

Media Influences: Television, movies, radio, and music all have profound influence on youth development. Before they are able to make their own judgments and value systems that will benefit them and society, they can be effected in a negative way by the pervasive glorification of drugs, sex, violence, and gang lifestyles.

Our youth today are crying out for understanding and guidance, but they must respect the giver before they can accept the offer. If they are not reached at an early stage of their social rebellion, the task can become very difficult...not impossible, but difficult. Some will be unreachable.

"Violence is part of life out here. In our 'hood you see violence all the time, and that's what time it is. Either you stay ready or it's gonna get you . . . To me, selling dope is the best thing a young girl can do in trying to make it in the streets. Call us a gang or whatever you want. What we is, is getting paid." Dewana, age 20, member of drug gang. From Washington State University Research, C. Taylor (1993) "Girls, Gangs, Women, and Drugs"

Why Join A Gang?
- Searches for love, structure, and discipline.
- A sense of belonging and commitment.
- The need for recognition and power.
- Companionship, training, excitement, and activities.
- A sense of self worth and status.
- A place of acceptance.
- A need for physical safety and protection.
- A family tradition or example set by parents, or guardians.

At the introductory phase of gang membership, the young person latches onto peers or older youths in the group that impresses them most. They can be impressed in many ways, dress, speech, walk, cars, or simply a sympathetic ear and an

understanding attitude. **They are most often impressed by the free and non-judgmental lifestyle and financial freedom. They are easily, sexually and emotionally controlled.** As gang association progresses, and what personal values they had declined, abandoning this environment and returning home is almost impossible, and as relationships and commitment deepen, attempting to leave a gang can be very dangerous, if not fatal (National Foundation For Abused And Neglected Children 1999).

WARNING TO PARENTS AND FAMILY MEMBERS: There are basic early warning signs and identifiers that might indicate gang affiliation, but you should exercise extreme caution, and do not be too quick to assume the worst in young people. The behavior and lifestyle that seem antisocial to you may just be adolescent phases that will one day run its course. It is called being a kid. However, with enough common denominators, adolescent social behavior, dress, peer interaction, and other unusual attitudes can be the first troubling signs of gang involvement. Be very careful how you handle these early symptoms. Seek professional counseling, and do not assume anything. When falsely accused, some young people pull away from those that lack trust and understanding, and gravitate toward gang activity out of misplaced spite and anger. If we read the signs wrong, a U-Turn is often difficult, if not impossible.

OUR YOUNG PEOPLE SHOULD BE TREATED LIKE MING CHINA, EXTREMELY DELICATE AND PRICELESS BEYOND VALUE.

The William Gladden Foundation, in their 1992 report, "The Reasons Why Gangs Form and Why Students Join Them," is reinforcement for our discussion to this point. The primary reason is that their needs are not being met elsewhere. The gangs give them the sense of family and acceptance they are lacking. Some are attracted because of strong ethnic identity. By understanding how gangs meet the needs of our children, we can make some real progress, and society will be better prepared to response in a meaningful way. Until that day comes, make no mistake about one thing, youth gangs are dangerous, and we need to know how to protect ourselves from becoming a target. I guess the Boy Scout Motto seems rather tame under these circumstances, but "Be Prepared" might be the best thing we can do until we get it right. Here are a few of the warning signs outlined by SEGAC, Southeastern Gang Activity Group. If one or more of these behaviors are evident, communication with your child is crucial to determine the level of involvement.

1. Your child admits to gang involvement.
2. Is obsessed with a particular color of clothing, or particular logo or tattoo.
3. Wears a style of clothing outside the norm.
4. Wears excessive jewelry beyond his or her financial means.
5. Wears jewelry or designs on only one side of the body.
6. Wears a cap or headband of a distinct color, or pattern.
7. Is obsessed with gangster-influenced music (Gangsta-Rap).
8. Becomes withdrawn from normal family activities.
9. Has a sudden change of demeanor, or aggressive attitude.
10. Associates with undesirables and breaks parental rules.
11. Develops an unusual need for privacy, or starts locking his or her bedroom door.
12. Uses computer chartrooms, and locks family out of computer activity with special password.
13. Uses special hand sign with friends.
14. Has unexplained cash or jewelry.
15. Shows signs of drug or alcohol use.

These are only a sampling of indicators that should be reasons for concern to parents and family members. Open a line of communication or seek professional help immediately.

Recommended Books:
Do or Die- by Leon Bing
There are no Children Here- by Alex Kotlowitz
My Posse Don't Do Homework-by LouAnne Johnson
Fist, Stick, Knife, Gun-by Geoffery Canada

Monster by Monster – by Kody Scott
Warriors Don't Cry – by Melba Pattillo Beals

VIDEOS YOU SHOULD SEE:
Boyz In The Hood
Blood In, Blood Out
South Central
Ain't No Denyin
Gangs and Violence In The 90's
(Strong Violence – Parental Supervision Advised)
"The Killing Fields of America" produced by CBS (To Order, Call 1-800-934-NEWS)
"Colors II" by Aurora Gang Task Force, Aurora, CO. (303) 695-2603
"What Can I Do About Violence" Produced by Bill Moyers, call 1-800-336-1917
"Gangs In School - Breaking Up Is Hard To Do" by the National School Safety Center, 16830 Ventura Blvd., Suite 200, Encino, California 91436

Gangs are competitive, territorial, and violent. When gang members are caught breaking the law they are tried in a court of law, and if convicted, they are punished according to the severity of the crime, just like any other criminal. Society pays the cost of these trials and incarcerations, but it is the victim that pays the price.

Many gang members, if not most, are by-products of inner-city poverty, and dysfunctional homes that have failed to provide structure and support. Single parent homes are a major contributor for their feeling of inferiority, uncertainty, and anger. Environmental conditions can twist and distort attitudes and behavior to such an extent that extraordinary acts of horror and violence become every day occurrences. But even seemingly solid middle and upper middle class two parent homes, well removed from poverty and despair, can produce monsters…remember "Columbine High School?"

To make a point, let us look in on a modest community, well removed from the crime-ridden streets of Chicago, New York, or Detroit.

RENO NEVADA, population 180,480 is known as "The Biggest Little City in the World." Located in the majestic Sierra Nevada Mountains, the breathtaking Reno-Sparks-Lake Tahoe area. It is a coveted vacation destination by world travelers. From the arts to the cultural splendor, from the world famous casinos to its unprecedented natural surroundings, Reno is truly a city offering a vibrant economy and excellent quality of life.

Nevertheless, like most cities in America, Reno has a dark side not found in the Chamber of Commerce brochures.

RENO POLICE DEPARTMENT CASE #140219-01 and WASHOE COUNTY SHERIFF'S CASE #140219-01
June 3, 2001

Approximately 10:10 p.m. RPD (Reno Police Department) responded to 1550 Locust Street on a report of several shootings. A 17 year old male juvenile was in front of this address when a vehicle drove up and a passenger in the vehicle fired approximately five shots from a handgun at the juvenile and then fled. The juvenile was not injured in the shooting. He was a known gang member and it is suspected that another rival gang member shot at him.

Approximately 10:23 p.m. RPD received numerous calls of shots fired in the area of 1360 Nannette Circle. A male subject was crossing the street when a white car pulled up and asked him what his gang affiliation was. This victim, who had no gang ties whatsoever, replied that he just lived in the area. One of the occupants of the vehicle then fired several shots at him, all of which missed.

Approximately 10:38 p.m. Washoe County Sheriff's responded to an address in Sun Valley in reference to a drive-by shooting with a suspect vehicle with a description similar to the first two shootings. No one was injured in this shooting.

Approximately 11:02 p.m. another drive-by shooting took place in front of 1510 Harvard Way. A vehicle was shot several times and again the same vehicle description as in the earlier shootings was seen leaving the area. No one was injured in this shooting. The owner of the vehicle does have gang affiliations. The suspect was described as a Hispanic male adult, 20's, 5ft.10in., medium build and wearing a white tank top and black pants. A mid 80's, white vehicle similar to a Chrysler has been seen at each instance. Reno Police Department Community Action Team has asked anyone with information to contact the Secret Witness Hotline at 322-4900.

The next time you are out walking in your neighborhood, sitting in the park, or quietly watching a movie, look around you. Anyone in close proximity, at any given time, has the potential to commit crime and violence. To think otherwise is a foolish exercise in fantasy. Denial won't keep you safe, but awareness and avoidance might. Always stay within your personal comfort zone whenever possible, and learn escape and evasion tactics when you are in a potentially dangerous situation. Don't take this lightly. Gangs can be very dangerous, and can be found in every state.

This is a list of Gangs. Not all, but just enough to get my point across. If you encounter these people, do not stick around for the thrill of association. They are not playing games. They are dead serious.

A number of visitors to Robert Walker's website, Gangs OR Us, have requested information concerning gangs in a particular state. As a courtesy, the information below is being provided for "HARD TARGET" readers. This state-by-state list is by no means a complete list of gangs that may be found in each state and is intended to serve only as an indicator of gang activity within each state. It also indicates how gangs by the same name have expanded and proliferated from state to state. **Only those gangs that may be well known within the region, or nationally, are listed; local gangs are too numerous.** Should you require specific information about gangs in your community, I suggest you contact your local, county, state law enforcement agency, or review Robert Walkers web site for additional information. www.gangsorus.com

Chapter Six   Gangs

Alabama
Bloods, Crips, Black Gangster Disciples, East Coast Crips, Insane Gangster Disciples, Playboy Gangster Crips, Skinheads
Gangs in Prison - Arizona Aryan Brotherhood, Vice Lords

Alaska
Bloods, Crips, Mara Salvatrucha, Tiny Rascal Gangsters
Gangs in Prison - Aryan Brotherhood, Black Gangster Disciples, La Raza, Skinheads

Arizona
Bloods and Crips (numerous sets of each), Brown Mexican Pride, Gangster Disciples, Latin Kings, Mau Mau, Nazi Low Riders, Norteños, Sureños. Wetback Power
Gangs in Prison - Arizona Aryan Brotherhood, Arizona's New Mexican Mafia, Arizona's Old Mexican Mafia, Aryan Brotherhood. Border Brothers, Mau Mau, Warrior Society

Arkansas
Bloods, Crips, Gangster Disciples, Mara Salvatrucha, Vice Lords
Gangs in Prison - Aryan Brotherhood

California
Ba Hala Na, Bloods and Crips (numerous sets of each), Black Gangster Disciples, Florencia 13, Norteños, Skinheads, Supreme White Power, Sureño 13, Tiny Rascal Gangsters, 18th Street
Gangs in Prison - Aryan Brotherhood, Black Guerrilla Family, Bloods, Bull Dogs (F-14), Crips, La Nuestra Familia, Mexican Mafia, Nazi Low Riders, Northern Structure, Texas Syndicate

Colorado
Aryan Brotherhood, Black Gangster Disciples, Bloods, Crips, (numerous sets of each) Mexican Mafia, Ku Klux Klan, Skinheads, Sureño 13, Tiny Rascal Gangsters, Vatos Locos, Vice Lords
Gangs in Prison - Aryan Brotherhood, Black Guerrilla Family, Dirty White Boys, La Nuestra Familia, Mexican Mafia, New Mexico Syndicate, Texas Syndicate

Connecticut
Latin Kings, La Ñeta, Los Solidos
Gangs in Prison - Aryan Brotherhood, La Ñeta, Latin Kings, Los Solidos

Delaware
Dog Pound

Chapter Six — Gangs

Gangs in Prison - Aryan Brotherhood, Latin Kings

Florida
Crips (numerous sets), Gangster Disciples, Insane Gangster Disciples, Latin kings
Gangs in Prison - Aryan Brotherhood, Black Gangster Disciples, Bloods, Crips, Five Percenters, Gangster Disciples, Insane Gangster Disciples, Jamaican Posse, La Familia, La Raza, Latin Kings, Skinheads

Georgia
Black Gangster Disciples, Bloods and Crips (numerous sets), Gangster Disciples, La Raza, Latin Kings, Mara Salvatrucha, Norteños, Sur 13, Sureños 13, Vice Lords
Gangs in Prison - Aryan Brotherhood, Black Gangster Disciples, Bloods, Crips, Five Percenters, Skinheads

Hawaii
Black Gangster Disciples, Hawaii Boys, Judas, Sons of Samoa
Gangs in Prison - Aryan Brotherhood, Black Gangster Disciples, Black Guerrilla Family, Bloods, Crips, Ku Klux Klan, La Nuestra Familia, Mexican Mafia, Skinheads, Vice Lords

Idaho
Black Gangster Disciples, Crips, Dog Pound, Skinheads, Sur 13, Sureño13, White Aryan Resistance
Gangs in Prison - Unknown

Illinois
Black Gangster Disciples, Black P Stones, El Rukns, Four Corner Hustlers, Gangster Disciples, Harrison Gents, Imperial Gangsters, Imperial Vice Lords, La Familia, La Raza, Latin Kings, Latin Queens, Maniac Latin Disciples, Mickey Cobras, Pachucos, Sisters of the Struggle, Sureños 13, Two Two Boys, Vice Lords
Gangs in Prison - Aryan Brotherhood, Black Gangster Disciples, El Rukns, Latin Kings, Mickey Cobras, Vice Lords

Indiana
Black Gangster Disciples, Black P Stones, Bloods, Crips, Four Corner Hustlers, Gangster Disciples, Ku Klux Klan, Latin Kings, La Raza, Mexican Mafia, Vatos Locos, Skinheads, Vice Lords
Gangs in Prison - Aryan Brotherhood, Black Gangster Disciples, Vice Lords

Iowa
Black Gangster Disciples, Black P Stones, Crips, El Rukns, Four Corner

Chapter Six   Gangs

Hustlers, Gangster Disciples, Insane Vice Lords, Ku Klux Klan, Latin Kings, Skinheads, Vice Lords
Gangs in Prison - Arizona Aryan Brotherhood, Aryan Brotherhood, Black Gangster Disciples, Crips, Dirty White Boys, Latin Kings, Vice Lords

Kansas
Asian Boyz, Black Gangster Disciples, Bloods, Crips (numerous sets), Four Corner Hustlers, Gangster Disciples, Insane Gangster Disciples, Latin Kings, Latin Queens, Norteños, Sureños 13, Vatos Locos, Vice Lords
Gangs in Prison - Aryan Brotherhood, Black Gangster Disciples, Bloods, Crips, Skinheads, Vice Lords

Kentucky
Asian Boyz, Black Gangster Disciples, Vice Lords
Gangs in Prison - Aryan Brotherhood, El Rukns, Gangster Disciples

Louisiana
Black Gangster Disciples, Bloods, Crips, Latin Kings
Gangs in Prison - Aryan Brotherhood, Bloods, Crips

Maine
Asian Boyz, Crips, Latin Kings, Tiny Rascal Gangsters
Gangs in Prison - Crips, Latin Kings

Maryland
Asian Boyz, Crips, Mara Salvatrucha, Skinheads
Gangs in Prison - Unknown

Massachusetts
Almighty Latin King & Queen Nation, La Familia, La Ñeta, Latin Kings, Los Solidos, Skinheads
Gangs in Prison - Aryan Brotherhood, Asian Boyz, Black Gangster Disciples, Black Guerrilla Family, Bloods, Crips, Five Percenters, Jamaican Posses, Ku Klux Klan, La Familia, La Nuestra Familia, Ku Klux Klan, Latin Kings, La Ñeta, Skinheads, Vice Lords

Michigan
Bloods, Crips, Gangster Disciples, Latin Kings, Tiny Rascal Gangsters, Vice Lords, Young Guns
Gangs in Prison - Latin Kings, Vice Lords, Young Guns

Minnesota
Bloods, Crips, Gangster Disciples, Latin Kings, Vice Lords
Gangs in Prison - Black P Stones, Bloods, Crips, Latin Kings, Vice Lords

Chapter Six — Gangs

Mississippi
Black Gangster Disciples, Black P Stones, Bloods, Crips, Conservative Vice Lords, Four Corner Hustlers, Gangster Disciples, Vice Lords
Gangs in Prison - Arizona Aryan Brotherhood, Black Gangster Disciples, Black P Stones, Bloods, Crips, El Rukns, Four Corner Hustlers, Simon City Royals, Vice Lords

Missouri
Aryan Brotherhood, Asian Boyz, Black Gangster Disciples, Bloods (numerous sets), Crips (numerous sets), Gangster Disciples, La Familia, Latin Kings, Mexican Mafia, Skinheads, Sureños 13, Vice Lords
Gangs in Prison - Unknown

Montana
Bloods, Crips, Gangster Disciples, Insane Gangster Disciples, Sureños
Gangs in Prison - Unknown

Nebraska
18th Street, Black Gangster Disciples, Bloods, Conservative Vice Lords, Crips, Gangster Disciples, La Raza, Latin Kings, Mara Salvatrucha, Mexican Mafia, Surenos 13,
Gangs in Prison - Aryan Brotherhood, Black Gangster Disciples, Crips, Latin Kings, Mexican Mafia

Nevada
Asian Boys, Ba Hala Na, Bloods, Crips, Latin Kings, Mara Salvatrucha, Mara Villa, Nazi Low Riders, Norteños, Skinheads, Sureños 13
Gangs in Prison - Aryan Brotherhood, Bulldogs (F-14), Crips, Gangster Disciples, La Nuestra Familia, Latin Kings, Mexican Mafia, Northern Structure

New Hampshire
Aryan Brotherhood, Black Gangster Disciples, Bloods, Crips, Latin Kings, Ñeta, Tiny Rascal Gangsters
Gangs in Prison - Aryan Brotherhood, Crips, Gangster Disciples, Latin Kings

New Jersey
Almighty Latin King and Queen Nation, Bloods, Crips, Dog Pound, Dominicans Don't Play, Five Percenters (5%), G 27, La Familia, Latin Kings, Los Solidos, MS 13, Ñeta, Vatos Locos, Zulu Nation
Gangs in Prisons - Aryan Brotherhood, Afrikan Liberation Army, Afrikan National Ujamaa, Black Gangster Disciples, Bloods, Conservative Vice Lords, Crips, Five Percenters, G-27, Ku Klux Klan, La Familia, Latin Kings, Ñeta, Skinheads

Chapter Six Gangs

New Mexico
Black Gangster Disciples, Bloods, Crips, Marielitos, Sureños
Gangs in Prison - 18th Street, Aryan Brotherhood, Bloods, Crips, New Mexico Syndicate, Sureños 13, Texas Syndicate

New York
Almighty Latin King and Queen Nation, Black Guerrilla Family, Bloods, Born to Kill, Crips, Five Percenters, Gangster Disciples, Jamaican Posse, La Familia, La Raza, Los Solidos, Mara Salvatrucha, Mexican Mafia, Ñetas, Supreme White Power, Toy Soldiers, Untouchables, Young Guns,
Gangs in Prison - Bloods, Five Percenters, Latin Kings, Ñetas

North Carolina
18th Street, Bloods, Crips, Gangster Disciples, Latin Kings,
Gangs in Prison - Aryan Brotherhood of Texas, Crips, Five Percenters, Gangster Disciples

North Dakota
Bloods, Crips, Sureños 13,
Gangs in Prison - Unknown

Ohio
Bloods, Conservative Vice Lords, Crips, Gangster Disciples, Insane Spanish Cobras, Ku Klux Klan, Latin Kings, Vice Lords,
Gangs in Prison - Arizona Aryan Brotherhood, Aryan Brotherhood, Black Gangster Disciples, Bloods, Crips, Five Percenters, Latin Kings, Mexican Mafia

Oklahoma
Aryan Brotherhood, Black Gangster Disciples, Bloods, Born To Kill, Confederate Hammerskins, Crips, Gangster Disciples, Insane Gangster Disciples, Jamaican Posse, Ku Klux Klan, Latin Counts, Latin Kings, Skinheads, Vice Lords, White Aryan Resistance
Gangs in Prison - Aryan Brotherhood, Bloods, Crips, Dirty White Boys, Gangster Disciples, Mexican Mafia, Mexikanemi

Oregon
Asian Boys, Black Gangster Disciples, Bloods, Crips, Gangster Disciples, Ku Klux Klan, Latin Kings, Mexican Mafia, Neo-Nazis, Norteños, Skinheads, Sureños, Varrio Locos
Gangs in Prison - Aryan Brotherhood, Bloods, Crips, Skinheads

Pennsylvania
Almighty Latin Kings Nation, Aryan Brotherhood, Asian Boyz, Bloods, Crips, Dog Pound, Five Percenters, Gangster Disciples, Ku Klux Klan, Skinheads,

Chapter Six — Gangs

Tiny Rascal Gangsters, Vatos Locos
Gangs in Prison - Aryan Brotherhood, Bloods, Crips, La Nuestra Familia, Latin Kings, Ñeta, Young Guns

Rhode Island
Street Gangs - Unknown
Gangs in Prison - Five Percenters, Latin Kings, Los Solidos

South Carolina
Almighty Latin Kings Nation, Aryan Brotherhood, Asian Boyz, Black Gangster Disciples, Black Mafia, Bloods, Brothers of the Struggle, Crips, Dirty White Boys, Five Percenters, Gangster Disciples, Insane Gangster Disciples, Ku Klux Klan, Mexican Mafia, Neo-Nazi, Nuestra Familia, Skinheads, Untouchables, Vatos Locos, Vice Lords, Young Guns
Gangs in Prison - Black Gangster Disciples, Black Mafia, Bloods, Crips, Five Percenters, Mexican Mafia, Young Guns

South Dakota
Bloods, Crips, Gangster Disciples
Gangs in Prison - Aryan Brotherhood, Black Gangster Disciples, Black P Stones, Bloods, Crips, Gangster Disciples, Ku Klux Klan, Latin Kings, Norteños 14, Skinheads, Sureños 13, Vice Lords

Tennessee
Black Gangster Disciples, Bloods, Confederate Hammerskins, Crips, Gangster Disciples, Imperial Vice Lords, Insane Gangster Disciples, Ku Klux Klan
Gangs in Prison - Aryan Brotherhood

Texas
Black Gangster Disciples, Bloods (numerous sets), Crips (numerous sets), Latin Kings, Mara Salvatrucha, Skinheads, Sureños 13, Untouchables,
Gangs in Prison - Aryan Brotherhood of Texas, Barrio Azteca, Black Gangster Disciples, Bloods, Crips, Hermanos Pistoleros Latinos, Latin Kings, Mandingo Warriors, Mexican Mafia, Raza Unida, Texas Mafia, Texas Syndicate

Utah
http://www.ci.logan.ut.us/police/gangproject/types.htm
18th Street, Asian Boys, Bloods, Crips, Gangster Disciples, Nortenos, Sinaloan Cowboys, Skinheads, Straight Edgers, Sureños 13, Tiny Rascal Gangsters, Vice Lords, White Supreme Power
Gangs in Prison - Aryan Brotherhood, Black Guerrilla Family, Mexican Mafia, Sureños 13

Vermont
Los Solidos
Gangs in Prison - Los Solidos

Virginia
Bloods, Crips, Insane Gangster Disciples, Mara Salvatrucha, Tiny Rascal Gangsters,
Gangs in Prison - 18th Street, Aryan Brotherhood, Black Gangster Disciples, Black Guerrilla Family, El Rukns, Five Percenters, Ku Klux Klan, La Nuestra Family, La Raza, Skinheads

Washington
18th Street, Black Gangster Disciples, Bloods, Crips, Ku Klux Klan, Mara Salvatrucha, Norteños, Skinheads, Sureños, Tiny Rascal Gangsters
Gangs in Prison - 18th Street, Aryan Brotherhood, Aryan Brotherhood of Texas, Black Gangster Disciples, Bloods, Bull Dogs (F-14), Crips, Gangster Disciples, Latin Kings, Mara Salvatrucha, Mexican Mafia, Northern Structure, Skinheads, Texas Syndicate, Vice Lords, White Aryan Resistance

West Virginia
Crips, Simon City Royals
Gangs in Prison - Unknown

Wisconsin
Black Gangster Disciples, Black P Stones, Bloods, Crips, Four Corner Hustlers, Gangster Disciples, Imperial Gangster Disciples, Latin King, Maniac Latin Disciples, Mickey Cobras, Orchestra Albany, Vatos Locos, Vice Lords,
Gangs in Prison - Aryan Brotherhood, Black Gangster Disciples, Black P Stones, Bloods, Crips, El Rukns, La Nuestra Familia, Latin Kings, Spanish Cobras, Vice Lords

Wyoming
Bloods, Crips, Skinheads
Gangs in Prison - Arizona Aryan Brotherhood, Aryan Brotherhood, Bloods, Crips, Mexican Mafia

If you see graffiti using any of these names, don't attempt to erase or paint over the names or any other symbols you may be offended by. If you feel they represent property damage, contact the local police gang unit before you destroy this "art-work." Gangs consider their names as a badge of honor, and will resort to extreme violence to protect that honor. Usually, by placing their names or symbols on walls and fences, they are marking their territory for other gangs, or anyone else, to publicly show this is their turf. It belongs to them! They rule!

If you see someone wearing clothing or tattooed with obvious gang names, or wearing colors or dress code signifying a gang, my best advice is to leave immediately. They are not interested in playing one-on-one basketball, they are not interested in joining your community car wash, and they are not the official greeters for the local mall. They are planning nothing with a social redeeming value, and approaching them with even casual conversation will often spark a violent confrontation. If trained social service agencies, law enforcement personnel, and a host of crime prevention researchers find these groups unapproachable, why would you approach them.

"Parents wonder why the streams are bitter, when they themselves have poisoned the fountain." — John Locke, 17th Century English Philosopher

CHAPTER SEVEN

Domestic Violence

I think that every reader will agree that our society and the world in general, can often be a dangerous place to live. As we have no other options at the moment, 'stop the world I want to get off' is certainly not a viable option. Awareness and avoidance is an attitude that should be adopted by everyone, not fear and worry, and not hiding from reality. Just awareness and avoidance, and a sensible crime management plan of action should we become a target for any type of crime or violence.

There is one arena of victimization that is significantly more complicated than a simple burglary, car theft, or robbery...domestic violence. Often referred to as the silent or hidden crime, domestic violence is primarily committed against women and children, although it is by no means exclusive to one specific gender. Domestic violence is a growing crime problem in the United States and is attracting the attention of media and government alike. Yet local and state government, doctors, lawyers, and educators all agree that this type of devastating social cancer is rapidly growing out of control and leaving a trail of carnage and destruction that is almost unimaginable in terms of pain and suffering, as well as huge financial losses. Irrespective of ethnicity, gender, sexual orientation, age or religion, all citizens should be made aware that denial, fear or hiding domestic violence will not make it go away. In fact, most experts feel that denial can even cause it to escalate to the ultimate crime of murder.

Chapter Seven — Domestic Violence

The Bureau of Justice Statistics estimates that over 960,000 incidents of domestic violence were reported in 2001, and worldwide it is estimated that one in three women will be assaulted, or sexually abused in her lifetime. Keep in mind that these statistics only reflect *reported* crimes, while the vast majority of domestic violence, encounters remain behind closed doors and are never reported.

Domestic violence is a very complex form of crime, but it is a crime, and should be a part of your personal safety strategy. By no stretch of the imagination can I call myself an authority on this subject, but extensive research tells me that there are options that can keep you from becoming a victim, or if you are already being victimized, you can do something about it. You are not helpless. You can break a pattern of coercive control by another. You can refuse to be a victim of domestic violence, but like any other crime, you need information and understanding of the problem before you can address the solution.

The first step in developing a safety strategy for domestic violence is to break the silence that surrounds this appalling social problem. One national organization, out of many, that has been an active voice in the national public policy arena on the issues of domestic violence is the Family Violence Prevention Fund headquartered in San Francisco, California. Over the last 20 years, the FVPH has served as a respected and reliable resource to members of congress, congressional committees, and the executive branch, and is considered by all crime prevention practitioners as one of the leading authorities in America on domestic violence.

Lynne Lee, FVPF Director of Public Education, has granted permission to use selected information from their extensive website for this chapter. I encourage every reader to log onto this site. The work and dedication of this organization impressed me. I will list complete contact information in the credit section. In the mean time, here is a gripping window into the world of domestic violence from those that have lived to tell the story, and some that have not.

Karen's Story

I myself am a survivor of domestic violence and can attest to the fact that individual people and their actions saved my life. I would like to share with you a little of my story to let you know that you can make a difference in the lives of people who are being abused. My ex-husband was violent to me for 2-1/2 years. Before getting married, we dated for 3 years, with no instances of violence. After our marriage, we moved from Virginia to Nashville TN, where he started work on a Ph.D.

The violence began within the first week of our marriage, where he pressed his hands against my mouth and nose attempting to smother me. After this incident, my ex-husband would become violent almost nightly often for no apparent reason. One of his favorite assaults was to strangle me with my back against the wall, my feet dangling a foot or so above the floor. He would get right into my face and scream, "What makes you think I won't kill you and then kill myself?" He would keep me up all night, often lecturing me endlessly and if I got sleepy he would attack me, often times choking me. I was in a constant state of exhaustion, sleeping an average of 2 hours a night.

His violence was controlled and directed at certain parts of my body so that the injuries were not visible to co-workers and friends. The welts from him hitting me were often on my head or torso, covered by my clothing. The only time that my bruises were visible was the fat lip from that very first bout of violence, where he pressed his hand against my mouth and nose, smothering me. Only one person asked me about my swollen lip and directly asked if my ex-husband had caused it. I was terrified that my husband would kill me if I told anyone, so I said no. This co-worker never again brought up the issue.

My ex-husband decided to transfer to a University in St. Louis. I was also hopeful that the violence would stop if he were happier in school. My hopes were dashed almost immediately. After one particularly awful episode of violence where he attacked me while I was sleeping, I got up very early the next morning and ran to our church, which was one block from our apartment. I talked to the priest and told him that I was afraid that my husband was going to "accidentally" kill me. He told me that the violence wasn't my fault and that I should leave.

During the last 2 years of our marriage, I tried to leave several times. Each time I attempted to leave, he would accelerate his violence. Once, I got as far as getting into my car, but he opened the car door before I could lock it. He bashed my head against the inside of the passenger door and dragged me screaming all the way down the block to our apartment. Not one of the hundreds of neighbors who heard me called the police, or ever asked me if anything was wrong.

Four months after visiting the priest, I got my courage up again to try to leave. I was on my way out the door to work when he begged me to stay home and threw me to the floor. I convinced him that we needed the money, so he let me go. Rather than return from work, I stayed in a shelter sponsored by my church. I called work and told them my situation. My supervisor was very supportive and gave me time off from work and wanted to know how she could help.

One week later, my ex-husband got into a serious car accident and begged me to return. He was very remorseful and made promises that he would change and get help through counseling. I returned to him, fueled by promises of change. Over time, however, these promises proved extremely empty. Slowly, he returned to using violence against me. The most memorable episode was on my last birthday with him, when he stood over me with an axe, threatening to kill me.

One month after this episode, he became violent one morning and began to choke me and then threw me to the floor. He then proceeded to literally walk on me. A light bulb went off in my head that he was actually walking on me like I was a rug. I thought, he's financially, psychologically, emotionally and now physically walking all over me. This was the final straw. I knew at that moment that I was going to leave him for good this time. Part of the reason that I knew I could successfully leave was because a woman with whom I worked was very open about her experiences with her violent ex-husband. Part of me knew that if she could do it, that I could do it too. I got up off the floor and ran to the car. This time I had enough time to lock my car door before he got to the car. I quickly drove away.

All I had with me were the clothes on my back, my purse, and the car. I stayed in an abused woman's shelter the first night and contacted work the next day. The response I received from my office was one of incredible support. I knew that my co-worker would understand my situation but I wasn't prepared for the generosity of my supervisor. They both met me for lunch and my boss took me to her house and gave me an adequate assortment of clothes to wear and told me to take off as much time as I needed. She also invited me to stay at her house, which I declined because I felt safer at the shelter for abused women.

I returned to work the following week and found numerous e-mail and voice mail messages from my ex husband. I got a restraining order on him and was helped by the campus security, which drove by my office around the time of my leaving to make sure I was safe. As time went by, I felt supported enough to tell my other co-workers, believing that the more people that knew my situation, the safer I was. I returned to school and was determined to stay in St. Louis and continue my life. However, because I had trouble renewing my restraining order, I again felt unsafe and I joined a friend in San Francisco.

It was the combination of many people over time that helped me to leave. Each person's statement and action contributed to my ability to leave. I remember the first co-worker in Nashville who asked me if my ex-husband caused my fat lip. He may have felt that it didn't do any good, or that he was wrong to ask. But by asking that question, it planted a seed in my mind that what was happening to me wasn't right.

I know it's frustrating to see people stay or go back to abusive relationships. However, there are many factors involved with staying and returning. The biggest factor for me was the fear for my life. I returned once because I still loved him, I loved the man that was my friend, who would go hiking with me, who would cook me dinner and comfort me when I was tired or sick. I loved the man who would play me music on his guitar, who would read me poetry, and who would tenderly tell me he loved me. I wanted to believe that man existed. But when his promises proved to be lies again and again, I was supported enough by other people in my life to see this and to leave.

I want to stress how terribly important the role that my co-workers played. True, I got support from the counselors at the abused women's shelter, but part of me felt they gave me the support because it was their job, unlike my co-workers who did it because they knew and cared for me. It wasn't because it was their job. I don't mean to say that the counselors weren't effective, they were. But it had even more impact on me when other people in my life gave me the same messages, that there was no excuse for my ex-husband's behavior, that not being happy at school, or our financial situation, nothing gave him the right to hit me.

If you are currently involved in a violent relationship, believe me, life can be better. You deserve it. I never thought I would enjoy life as much as I do now, unhindered by a constant threat of violence. I am working successfully and have joined the Advisory Committed of the Funds Survivors Mobilization Program.

The Family Violence Prevention Fund's campaign, "There's No Excuse for Domestic Violence" carries this same message. You can participate by endorsing and promoting this message - "There is never an excuse for Domestic Violence."

If you know someone who is being abused, or is abusive, you can help. Please call 1-800-END ABUSE. When you call this number, you'll receive a kit that will tell you specifically how to help someone who is being abused or whom you suspect is being abusive. You can make a difference. Act now. Call 1-800-END-ABUSE.

Paul's Story

Our experience began with the sound of 100 clicks. The phone in the office would ring; we'd say hello; there would be a short silence, then a click. It would happen ten times in a row, sometimes a hundred times a day.

Very soon after this began, Molly (not her real name) told us it was her former boyfriend, the father of her one-year-old child. She had told him not to call her or try to see her, but the message wasn't getting through.

Other incidents followed. He would park in front of the door waiting for her, and one day he confronted her in the doorway and tried to force her to come with him. Two people from another office in the building were there to help her that day, but things began to escalate after that.

As the director of our office, I don't remember making a conscious decision to support Molly - she was part of our team, and we all assumed that we would try to help. And once it was clear that our goal was to help, her interests became our interests.

She was shook up by the phone calls - we found them intolerable in a business, and made it clear to the caller that he'd never get through to her. She couldn't concentrate on her work, and her mistakes weren't helping us; we twice gave Molly extra paid leave to sort things out. The threat to her was a threat to everyone in the building, and we distributed a warning flyer with his picture. We introduced her to a counselor and started cooperating with the police and courts in her attempts to file and enforce a restraining order.

I wish I could say that was the end of it. One weekend, he left a series of obscene messages on our voice mail, threatening both Molly and her co-workers. We saved a tape of the messages, and this was crucial evidence for a violation of the restraining order.

In the end, Molly's harasser learned that his actions had consequences; Molly learned that she could rely on a network of support, and we learned that you can step forward and make a difference.

Remarks by Gayle Nicolson
From Alameda, California:

I feel that it is a tribute to my daughter and grandson to be here today to tell their story because this past Sunday, May 21st marked the third anniversary of their death. My daughter Nicole and three-year-old grandson Warren were stabbed to death in their own home. The murderer was not a stranger, but John Hoffman, my grandson's father. The effect this act of violence has had on our family cannot be put into words, and the wounds we have been left with cannot be seen, but they are there, and they will never go away.

Our grief is made even worse because of the guilt. The reason for the guilt is that we were with Nicole and Warren almost every day, but did not know of the violence that they were suffering at the hands of John. But there was one person who did know, and that person was Dawn Girard, a family law Judge.

We knew that she did not want a relationship with John and that she had been trying to move on with her life without him, but it was particularly hard for her because she wanted her son to have his father in his life. This wasn't good enough for John, he wanted her and his son. He was constantly harassing her and generally intruding on her life. We suggested that she get a restraining order and set up a place where John could have supervised visits with Warren without involving her. She agreed that this was the best course of action. She sat in my house and very carefully wrote a request for a restraining order. She asked me not to read what she had written. She said it was very hard for her to write but she knew it was time to take some action. She wanted to handle it through the legal system on her own.

I truly believe that if the court had been more sensitive to her request for help, I would not be standing here telling their story today.

We found out the details of what had been happening to her by reading her request for a restraining order on the front page of a local newspaper the day after the murders. At first, we considered the news article to be a thoughtless invasion of our family's privacy, but it has turned out to be an awakening and has given me a purpose and a reason to go on. That purpose is to see that all judges that preside in family courts are trained to recognize the signs of battered women, and be sensitive to their needs.

On May 1, 1992, Nicole stood in front of Judge Dawn Girard with a restraining order request that told of rape, beatings, child abuse, and numerous threats of death to her, her child, and her family. The following are a few direct quotes from that document.

"Starting over 4 years ago, John Hoffman has been acting out sexual and physical abuse. He has regularly beaten me and has made several threats to kill me. He has forced me to perform sexual acts despite desperate pleas to leave me alone. He also has made threats to harm my family and destroy their property if I leave him or call the police. He has injured Warren by slapping him, causing a blackened eye and welts on his face and head. I was severely beaten, almost strangled, and left with black eyes and bruises all over my body. These are not necessarily the worst things that John Hoffman has done to us, just examples of his capability of injuring me and my son. The fear my son and I have lived in has been horrible. I am terribly afraid of him and I need protection." However, she left that courtroom without a signed order.

The newspaper headline read that Nicole had dropped the restraining order. I could not understand why she would have dropped the order when there was no other reason for her to go to court that morning. After obtaining and reading the transcript, I became aware that the sense of resolve and confidence that Nicole had that morning was stripped away after having to stand beside a man she feared and testify to a Judge that had neither the sensitivity nor the interest to concern herself with the seriousness of the situation. The very first thing the Judge said was "Is everything you wrote in your application true and correct to the best of your knowledge and belief? Or do you want to drop this today?" Those words, "Or do you want to drop this today?" haunt me. I am at a loss to understand how one in a Judge's position could not see the obvious fact that Nicole and Warren were in mortal danger from this man. It is clear from reading the transcript that it was not Nicole who made the decision to drop the restraining order, but the influence of the Judge's authority.

It is the duty of family court Judges to act in the best interest of those who come before them seeking help. If Nicole had been listened to and taken seriously and able to plead her case in a more sympathetic and understanding environment, perhaps she would have felt more empowered, knowing that she could make a difference in protecting herself and her child through the court system, which is the only legal means that exists to protect victims like Nicole and Warren.

The manner in which the civil courts deal with domestic violence is in serious need of reassessment. We need mandatory intensive training and new policies for all levels of personnel who deal with families in crisis. Battered women have to be recognized and handled properly in the courts. Their cries for help must be taken seriously and the batterers must not be let off lightly.

There is nothing more that can be done for Nicole and Warren, but it is my deepest wish that by telling their story I might, in some small way, help change our legal system so that tragedies such as mine are averted in the future.

(As told at a Family Violence Prevention Fund Press Conference, San Francisco, CA, May 25, 1995).

These stories illustrate clearly that domestic violence can be recognized from behavior used to establish power and control through physical battering, fear, and intimidation. Assault, battering and psychological violence are criminal by nature. As I mentioned before, these are complicated crimes. There is sometimes no physical battering, but the victim is abused by psychological or mental assault that can be just as devastating as physical battering. In cases of physical battering, the perpetrator can exhibit behavior ranging from minor abusive contact, to violent murder. Another aspect of domestic violence is sexual abuse. Many times a physical attack will culminate in violent, unwanted sexual intercourse.

The Many Faces of Battery

- **Physical Assault**
  Physical violence may just start as simple shoving and pushing, but clearly evidence shows this can quickly escalate into slapping and hitting, choking, kicking, striking with objects or clubs, and use of knives and guns. Physical abuse often results in throwing a spouse or child down stairs, out of moving vehicles, or in front of a moving vehicle. Most domestic violence begins with threats and name-calling, or anger toward a child or family pet, and then evolves into behavior that is more aggressive until it becomes life threatening. Do not wait until the life threatening stage. Seek advice or counseling at the very first sign of aggressive attitude by your spouse. Alcohol and drugs play a prominent roll in domestic abuse cases.

- **Sexual Abuse**
  Domestic abuse often culminates in sexual violence, rape, unwanted abnormal sexual activity, and forced sexual activity with other family members or strangers as a means of humiliation and degradation by the abuser. Drugs and alcohol are often present.

- **Psychological Battering**
  This form of battery can be especially harmful, and often leaves the victim with a feeling of hopelessness and despair. A constant barrage of verbal assault on self-worth, excessive harassment toward children or friends, isolation from friends and family members, deprivation of physical and economic resources, and turning family and friends away from the victim

through lies and false accusations that demean or attack the honest and integrity. An early warning sign of domestic problems, although not necessarily violence, is a showing of extreme highs and lows, or marked mood swings. The psychological abuser will often show pleasure in making his victim do something distasteful or against their will. He can be unrealistically jealous, throw fits of temper, and express an overly possessive attitude, resulting in full-blown domestic violence.

- **Economic**
Economic abuse can be extremely cruel because it holds you hostage to the will and control of the abuser, just as surely as a set of chains. It is controlling and demeaning and robs you of the freedom of choice, movement, and worth. When battery starts, the victim often feels trapped because she has no financial options, and is left with a defeated attitude and submission. Many case studies show the abused spouse has no credit of their own, nothing in their name, like the car, house or bank accounts. In view of their situation, they feel trapped and helpless, and generally submit to abuse in the hope that they can change the attitude of the abuser—which is nothing more than an exercise in futility.

- **Threats**
The domestic violence abuser will have very strong traditional views regarding the roll of the male and the female in a domestic relationship. If the abuser is a male, and they most often are, he will show a controlling attitude. He will build a climate of fear, there will be vague threats or open warnings of great bodily harm, and even death. The victims will often look for ways to please the abuser to relieve the pressure and fear of threat. The more they succumb to intimidation by threat, the more they feed the ego and quest for power sought by the abused. It can only get worse unless the chain is broken. Don't become entangled in that chain until it takes you to the bottom of your well of despair.

Chapter Seven — Domestic Violence

- **FACT: Domestic violence is the most common and unrecognized killer of women in the United States. It kills more women than traffic accidents, muggings, and rapes combined.**

- **Acts of domestic violence occur every 18 seconds in America.**

- **95% of all domestic violence is women and children.**
- **Men commit over 95% of spousal abuse.**

- **Authorities estimate that husbands and boyfriends beat over 6 million American women each year.**

- **Domestic violence occurs equally across all sectors of society. It knows no social, economic, racial or religious boundaries.**

DOMESTIC VIOLENCE OFTEN THRIVES IN SILENCE ... AND OFTEN CARRIES OVER TO OUR CHILDREN.

A recent Bureau of Juvenile Justice article shows approximately one in five female high school students report being physically and/or sexually abused by a dating partner.

The Kaiser Permanente Poll

Children show 40% of girl's age 14 to 17 report knowing someone their age that has been hit or beaten by a boyfriend.
The Center For Research Policy revealed that during the 1996-1997 school year, there were an estimated 4,000 incidents of rape or other types of sexual assaults in public schools across America (and these are not taking into account all that we don't know that goes on behind the closed doors of silence).
IT'S NOT COMPLICATED...MONKEY SEE, MONKEY DO!

BREAKING THE CYCLE OF VIOLENCE

- Primarily, if you are in a relationship with someone who is abusing you, or you believe abuse is on the way, do not leave this book where he can find it. As a matter of common sense, do not even have this book in the house. Read it at work, or a friend's house. The mere presence of a book of this nature can become the spark to set the controller's mind on fire. Read it, and anything else you can get your hands on, but do so in private and without the knowledge of the person in question. As I've said before, you need good information to make good decisions, but just like a good boxer, don't telegraph your punches.

- Make a contingency plan in the event you have to leave the house quickly, or with very short notice. This should include pre-established friends or family that is willing to provide emergency shelter for you and any children. Become knowledgeable about restraining orders, and domestic violence counselors in your area.

- Recognize that it is happening to you.

- Accept that you are not to blame.

- Seek help and support immediately.

If you are currently in a dangerous situation, and have no doubt about it, domestic violence is a very dangerous situation. You might start making a survival package and leave it with a trusted friend, or safety deposit box known only to you.
1. Money and credit cards.
2. Personal identification (an abuser will often destroy your I.D. as another control play).
3. Social Security card and Birth Certificate. If you can't safely stash these items, make copies for easy renewal.

4. Children's school and health records.
5. Vehicle title and registration.
6. Green card or applicable permits.
7. Insurance information
8. Mortgage papers.
9. Family and friend address book.
10. Valuable jewelry.
11. Small items of emotional value.
12. Don't forget a favorite toy for a child that might be headed for a very stressful situation.
13. A diary chronicling abuse events would be invaluable for a divorce lawyer, but I realize this is not always practical or easy to do. Possibly just noting the time and date of each incident would help. If an injury occurred, keep copies of the medical records (in my opinion, don't wait for a second violent encounter. Leave him immediately after the first abuses...don't go back).

Nobody should let anyone assault or humiliate him or her. The abused is responsible for their actions - you are not at fault. A crime has been committed and you *are* entitled to the full protection under the law. You do not have to be a victim without recourse.

I encourage you to take a proactive approach to this problem. If you need help, or you suspect a friend or family member is in harm's way, do something positive before it is too late. Contact a friend for advice and support, bring your concerns to your pastor, call the local police or sheriff's department and ask to speak with the victim advocates officer. Please, don't let fear, self-doubt, or apathy make you or someone you care for a victim of this heartbreaking crime.

Additional Resources:
Family Violence Prevention Fund
383 Rhode Island Street, Suite 304
San Francisco, CA 94103-5133

(407) 252-8900
URL: http://www.fvpf.org/
National Organization for Victim Assistance (NOVA)
1 800 TRY-NOVA
WEB: http://www.try-nova.org/
National Crime Prevention Council
(202) 466-6272

National Clearinghouse for the Defense of Battered Women
(215) 351-0010
National Coalition on Domestic Violence
(303) 839-1852
National Domestic Hotline
1 800 709-SAFE
Staff provides callers with crisis intervention information about domestic violence, and referrals to local programs 24 hours a day, 7 days a week.

Personal safety and freedom from domestic violence begins with a state of mind, and an unshakable resolve to make changes. Creating a safe environment, free from the terror of battery has great value, and when you have something of great value you take special care to protect it. When you protect something of value it lasts a long time. Safety should be a long-term goal. Don't allow anyone to rob you of your dreams and contaminate the quality of your life. You have options. You can refuse to be a victim.

CHAPTER EIGHT

Senior Citizen Crime Prevention

Awareness/Avoidance and Safety Strategies are probably your three most important survival factors. Law enforcement, the military, and all crime prevention practitioners worldwide are of one accord when it comes to crime prevention — Awareness/Avoidance and Safety Strategies work! Being aware of your environment, avoiding confrontation, and pre-planning a personal safety strategy, should it ever be needed, can make the difference between property loss and even life and death. That said, clearly, it is well worth some serious thought and preparation. Becoming a crime victim is not difficult. The easiest way to accomplish this is to let apathy rule common sense. I've said it before, but it is worth repeating — many victims simply have a mindset that crime and violence would never happen to them. I've heard it so many times;

- Why would anyone bother me, I don't have anything?
- I'm not worried, we live in a gated community.
- We live in a neighborhood watch community.
- I haven't had a problem in 70 years, why worry about it now?
- I do not need an alarm, we have a dog.
- I only shop in the good part of town.
- I have a gun.
- We have a good police department.

- I take martial arts classes.
- The Lord protects me.

If you are one of those citizens that think crime will only happen to the *other* person and not you think about this…to the other person, you *are* the other person.

➢ Be aware of your surroundings.
➢ Be prepared for the possibility of danger.
➢ Establish your own personal comfort zone.
➢ Let your intuitions be your guide.
➢ Develop the resources to recognize and react to adverse situations.
➢ Make a decision to refuse to be a victim, and build a plan around that decision.

While this is primarily a book that focuses on keeping you safe from crime and violence, and much of the content deals with uncomfortable subject matter, it is well to remember that as people grow older, their chance of being a victim of crime decreases dramatically. But for some, life experiences, physical limitations, aging, and isolation often leave elder Americans feeling helpless and afraid.

This book mentions many organizations that are eager to assist those in need. Let them know you or someone you know needs advice and guidance. In reality, the greatest crime threat to seniors is when they view themselves as helpless. Don't let anything or anybody rob you of your golden years. You can refuse to be a victim.

Change has a considerable psychological impact on the human mind. To the fearful, it is threatening because it means that things may get worse. To the hopeful, it is encouraging because things may get better. To the self-confident, it is inspiring because the challenge exists to make things better. - King Whitney, Jr.

A recent study released in January 2001 by the Justice Department indicates that senior citizens, age 65 and older, are 10 times less likely than other age groups to be victimized by violent crime. The study shows some significant variation for Blacks, Hispanics, and male elderly. The study did not include nursing home or assisted care facilities. The majority of crimes reported by seniors were property type offenses, such as burglary, car theft, fraud, or deceptive trade practices. But a lifetime of problems associated with aging often makes older Americans fearful. Although they are constantly on the lookout for physical attack and home burglary, they are not as alert to frauds and con games, which is the greatest threat to seniors.

We don't live in a bubble, and all of use can expect to encounter the dark side of life from time to time…that's why we plan! But when you take a closer look at these statistics, it does not paint such a rosy crime reduction picture. As I've said before, crime and violence is in the DNA of our society, and the elderly are often targeted.

- ❖ On average, 1992-1997, for every 1,000 persons at their age level, person's age 65 or older experienced about 5 violent crimes while those younger than age 25 experienced over 100.
- ❖ Between 1992 and 1997, the average population of people age 65 or older was 31.3 million. These elderly were victims of 2.7 million properties and violent crimes, either completed or attempted.
- ❖ 2.5 million property crimes (household burglary, motor vehicle theft, and simple household theft).
- ❖ 46,000 purse snatchings or pocket pickings.
- ❖ 165,000 non-lethal violent crimes (rape, robbery, and aggravated and simple assault).
- ❖ 1,000 murders.

As science and medicine increases the senior population and demographics, the safety needs grow expediently. As the needs of elderly are often unique, their safety is of great concern to families, social service professionals, and law enforcement agencies. To meet these needs, education and training programs have never been more focused, and intervention efforts are available in even the smallest communities.

Although many family members, as well as social service agencies, clearly recognize the vulnerability of seniors, one factor remains a difficult barrier; Independence. Many seniors are staunchly independent, fixed in their ways, and very reluctant to admit their venerability. To compound that, most are simply nice people, with friendly trusting natures. Nice, friendly, polite and trusting, is what every thief hopes for…an Easy Target. The bad guys use many terms to describe their victims. Rube, gofer, mark, patsy, pigeon, john, targets. They all mean the same — an easy person to rob and cheat. While many excellent safety and security, awareness programs are freely available, getting some seniors to admit they need outside advice and assistance to remain safe is often difficult. Dignity and privacy are a big part of the problem.

As I've mentioned before, there is no honor among thieves, and little or no compassion for their victims. Crimes like Social Security fraud, telemarketing scams, various consumer swindles, burglary, home invasion, robbery and assault…and yes, even rape and murder are sad realities.

Planning starts with family and friends. If you have an elderly family member, talk with them about avoidance and awareness, even though that may be difficult. You, as a family member or friend, have a moral obligation to obtain and share information that can keep them out of harm's way.

If you are a senior citizen, and have no family or close friends, contact the National Sheriff's Office or the AARP and ask for help. One call is all it will take and thousands of members can be your extended family, willing and ready to provide support. These organizations, and hundreds like them, were formed for people just like you. Many senior citizens are taking a more proactive role in their safety, and the safety of their neighbors. Unfortunately, too many are locking themselves in, afraid and confused, ripe opportunities for predators. Many times we allow ourselves to become a victim simply because we are so good at it. Trust your intuitions, and do not ignore the warning signals the good Lord placed in all of us. That gift of intuition is one of our most powerful internal resources.

While statistically, senior citizens have a generally lower risk of becoming a victim, it is troubling to find that in seniors who were victims of violence, in 25% of those cases, the attacker was related to the victim, or was a trusted caregiver. When you make your strategic safety plan, keep in mind that violence is in all of us, and all that changes is how we justify that action. A person's intent of committing an act of crime cannot always be identified in advance, but their actions and your intuitions will often provide the early warning signals that will keep you safe.

As the graying of America continues, and the senior citizens are living longer, this should be their time to relax for a well-earned rest, and live out those twilight years with dignity and safety. Unfortunately, this is not always the case. By the very nature of the aging process, they present an easy target for those that choose to rob and cheat. Therefore, because we know this up front, I think it is time to help our aging loved ones develop a personal safety plan. To fail to address this obligation is unconscionable.
The plan begins here:
A. Awareness
B. Avoidance
C. Self-confidence
D. Support

Awareness is not complicated to understand or difficult to implement. Do you remember those early warnings from our parents about crossing a railroad track? Stop! Look! Listen!

Awareness is simply stopping for a moment to assess the situation. Trust those wonderful God-given intuitions to help make critical decisions. If you have a "gut" feeling that not all is right...it is probably not all right, and you should back away. One of the universal hungers is the hunger to feel safe. You have the manna within you to feed this hunger.

Avoidance is easy. If your sixth sense tells you that something is wrong, trust that feeling, and avoid that which seems uncomfortable. Establish a personal comfort zone that gives you the feeling of safety. A foot, three feet, or even arm's length. Whatever makes you feel comfortable. Then do not let strangers inside your comfort zone. When you see something potentially dangerous or threatening, go the other way. *Do not* continue toward what appears to be a danger zone, and expect to be unaffected by crime and violence.

Self-confidence: We are often unsure, or lack confidence in ourselves when we are dealing with adversity or the unknown. Once you understand why people act as they do, we will automatically find ourselves feeling more confident in dealing with them. Various scientific studies have proven that if you learn what makes the other person tick, you are now in control of the high ground. To make yourself "crime resistant" you must not only know what to do, but why you are doing it. Then, and only then, will you wear a cloak of self-confidence with ease and comfort.

Support: Senior citizens often find themselves living an isolated lifestyle. Spurned or ignored by family and relatives, loneliness and uncertainties can build powerful fears that most find unimaginable. No longer surrounded with children and laughter, now quietly retired from an active career, deep hidden fears of crime and violence begin to surface, along with a realization that they are vulnerable and afraid. It is with this knowledge that crime prevention practitioners like myself are eager to assist seniors. We can't bring back their youth, but we can offer help to ensure the quality of your future. Seniors and family alike should read the suggestions that follow. We can make a difference, but a collective effort can erect a giant wall of confidence and safety, and *really* make a significant difference. Remember that the youth of today are the senior citizens of tomorrow…it goes by faster than you think.

"Help someone today because turn-about is fair play."

Safety Strategies

➤ The first thing to do before planning anything is to talk about your concerns for safety with your family and friends. Ask them for advice. If no family members are available, talk with your local law enforcement agency. They all have excellent senior citizen crime prevention programs, and they are eager to address your concerns and offer professional advice. If you have a neighborhood watch program in your community, talk with them. If not, call your local sheriff's office and ask about establishing a neighborhood watch program provided by the National Sheriff's Association.

➤ Most study polls show that the fear of crime ranks as one of the chief concerns of senior citizens. However, this fear and concern can be healthy if it motivates you to take a proactive approach to crime and violence. A good, positive attitude and a crime management approach to your concerns can greatly reduce your chances of becoming a victim. After all, crime prevention is nothing more than recognizing criminal opportunity and doing something constructive to reduce or eliminate that opportunity. Putting it another way, we can discourage criminal activities when we have good prevention information. Like the Boy Scouts, be prepared.

Home security was covered in some detail in Chapter Five, and would apply to families or seniors, with these few additional precautions more specifically directed toward senior citizens.
- First, establish a locked door policy with your home and vehicle.
- Strengthen your doors and secure hinges better.

Chapter five covers doors in more detail. Statistical data tells us that somewhere between 70 and 80% of all burglars come through doors that are not adequately reinforced, or not secured properly. In fact, many doors are simply left unlocked. Well, in my opinion, leaving a door unlocked or poorly secured is like playing a game of Russian roulette...and that game can turn ugly in a heartbeat. If you take some time to address the issue of proper door security, you can reduce your chances of becoming a victim dramatically, and that's what this book is all about. Please take me seriously.
- Secure all windows.
- Install a burglar/fire alarm.
- Use caller I.D.
- Don't talk to strangers.

Senior citizens are generally trusting in nature. This, more than anything else, opens a window of opportunity for predators. Criminals prey on the elderly because they are easy targets, and they offer little threat of resistance. Over 600,000 prisoners are released every year, and the vast majority will commit more crimes. Can you tell the difference from a law-abiding citizen and a criminal? I cannot. Use caution and common sense when talking with a stranger, in person or on the phone.

- Carry a cell phone.

When it comes to security, cell phones are the next best things to cold meatloaf sandwiches. As an example, let us suppose that some moderately professional burglar enters your home in the middle of the night. You wake from a sound sleep and hear someone moving about your home. After that first flush of panic and fear, you hold your breath and listen carefully, heart pounding wildly, as you assure yourself you are not having a nightmare. Then, convinced that you have an unwanted intruder in your home, you quietly reach for the telephone on your nightstand, panic and apprehension raising in your throat like bile, and dial 911...the line is dead. Was this intruder sophisticated enough to cut the phone lines before entry? I doubt it. What a more experienced thief will do, immediately upon access, is take the first phone he sees off the hook. The moment that phone is taken off the hook; no phone in the house can be used. On the other hand, if your personal security plans calls for putting your cell phone on the nightstand upon retiring at night, you will always have emergency access to 911. You may never have an intruder in your home, but why tempt fate? It takes so little effort to adjust your lifestyle, and it might even help you get a good night's rest. If you don't have a cell phone hooked to a service, get a used one from a garage sale or pawn shop, plug it in with a power adapter, and take some comfort that all cell phones, hooked to a service or not, can dial 911. I talk about this in other chapters, and it is worth repeating because I care about you.

This may sound like I'm trying to scare you, but I'm not. My goal is to leave an indelible imprint on certain potential crime scenarios, and give you some options that will help you move beyond fear and panic. Remember, when you do not pre-plan, you open a door of opportunity to be victimized. Close that door!

❏ Small dogs are excellent early warning alarms.

Not only are dogs a good early warning system, they offer great companionship for seniors living alone. As the bond forms between owner and pet, the pet will become very protective and sensitive to his environment. A side benefit is the health aspects. Stress reduction and lower blood pressure are just a couple of proven benefits that make pet ownership something of value to be considered.

❏ Big dogs can be a liability and somewhat difficult for seniors to manage and care for.

Not only are big, vicious dogs a high liability for homeowners, they are not very effective against a seasoned criminal. Think about this. Dogs breathe through their mouths. If a burglar sprays the dog directly in the mouth with a cheap can of lacquer based hair spray, it will immediately disable the animal, and in fact, might even be fatal. Food for thought: If dogs worked, banks would have dogs.

❏ Quality auto alarm with remote panic button.

❏ Trim shrubbery from around windows.

If you have large shrubs that block the windows, it also affords a perfect hiding place for someone attempting entry through a window. Cut the shrubbery back and you make it more difficult for someone to rob you.

❏ Pull shades at night.

❏ Install a wide-angle peephole in front and back doors, and never open to strangers.

❏ Post-emergency numbers by the phones.

❏ Keep valuables in bank safe deposit box.

❏ Have friend or family check on you each evening.

❏ When working in yard, keep alarm remote with you.

Keeping your home alarm in your pocket when working in the yard, or relaxing on the patio can be extremely valuable as a deterrent. If you are approached be an unwelcome intruder, your remote control can activate your alarm, and alert neighbors that a potentially dangerous situation exists. In most cases, simply setting off the burglar alarm will send the bad guy running. It is also guaranteed to make the hair stand up on an unwanted salesperson that will not take no for an answer.

❏ When shopping, take a friend.

❏ Establish a personal comfort zone.

- Walk and park in well-lit areas.

- Keep keys in hand for quick access when entering your home or vehicle.

- If followed, drive to a public place or police station.

- If disabled, use your cell phone.

- If threatened, activate your auto or home alarm. In the case of a vehicle, holding the horn on is an excellent way to draw attention to a potential problem, and will generally send the would-be attacker running, while alerting others that you need help.

- Maintenance workers and repair crews must provide proper I.D. If in doubt, call the company.

- Install exterior lighting.

- Never hide keys outside, or under car bumpers.

These are only a few suggestions for personal safety. Not every tip will apply to everyone, nor can every senior citizen afford all of the security technology mentioned. But if you only do ten percent of these suggestions, your safety will be greatly improved. The more you do, the greater your security. As we continue to list security options, consider your personal concerns, as well as your budget, and try to incorporate as many of these suggestions as possible, as budget allows. You might check with your local sheriff's office, or city police. Many departments now have community safety officers that will assist you in developing a comprehensive safety plan.

Better Business Bureau:
The BBB is an excellent "free" resource for consumer guidance, business advice, dispute resolution, as well as information on

frauds and charities.

Call your local BBB office for information and free brochures available for senior consumers. If you have a computer, the BBB on-line program is easy to use and invaluable. FOREWARNED IS FOREARMED.

AARP: American Association of Retired Persons
Older Americans are the targets of choice for telemarketing fraud, and deceptive trade practices throughout our country. Fraudulent telemarketers are increasing at an alarming rate, stealing the life savings of our seniors, leaving many unsuspecting elders in financial ruin.
The United States Department of Justice estimates that one out six consumers is falling prey to telemarketing criminals every year, and those numbers are rapidly growing annually. With more than **10,000 fraudulent telephone operations in the United States**, hundreds of thousands of seniors are assaulted every year.
Congress estimates the consumer **cost of telemarketing crime at $40 billion**, and growing every year, and those costs only reflects the crimes that were reported. Some of the phone scams are so sophisticated that their victims never know they've been duped, while others fail to report the crime out of fear of being ridiculed by friends and family.
If you, or someone you know, suspect they have been victimized by telemarketing fraud, contact the **Federal Trade Commission** at **1-877-FTC-HELP**.

Here is a short list of some of the more prevalent phone scams listed with the AARP Web Site,
http://www.aarp.org/fraud/home.htm
1. Bank Examiner Scams
2. Credit Card Fraud
3. Door-to-Door Sales
4. Charity Fundraising
5. Home Improvement Fraud
6. Identity Theft
7. Telephone Cramming

8. The "Pigeon Drop" Scam
9. Medicare Fraud
10. Sweepstakes Action
11. Scholarship Scams
12. Travel Fraud
13. Vacation Plan Scam
AND THE LIST GOES ON, AND ON, AND ON...

Include fraudulent telemarketing crime in your personal safety strategies. Crime, in any form, can be defeated with good information and a good crime management approach. Decide how you are going to handle these phone calls in advance. Make a plan not to be a victim.

Personally, I use caller ID, and whenever the display says "caller unknown," or I can't identify the phone number, I let the answering machine pick up. If it is a telephone solicitation, any telephone solicitation, I erase it. I have a firm policy of not listening to a phone pitch, and I never commit to anything by telephone...period!

If you should receive a call, and you are suspicious, or your intuition sends out warning signals indicating this call is some kind of scam, hang up and call the sheriff's office and make a report. If your caller ID saves the number, include that in your report.

Albert Einstein once said, "The world is a dangerous place to live, not because of the people who are evil, but because of the people who don't do anything about it." Get involved. Be proactive. Refuse to be a victim!

Does Your Community Have A Triad Program?
The American Association of Retired Persons (AARP), The International Association of Chiefs of Police (IACP), and the National Sheriffs' Association (NSA) sponsor the Triad program on a national scale. Triad promotes partnerships between senior citizens and the law enforcement community, both to prevent crime against the elderly and to help law enforcement benefit from the talents of older people. If you are interested, contact your chief

of police, sheriff, or AARP chapter. For more direct information, call Triad at The National Sheriff's Association, 703-836-7827, or contact NATI, The National Association of Triads, Inc. at 860-675-4799.

YOU HAVE THE RIGHT NOT TO BE A VICTIM !

For information on senior crime prevention programs in your area, contact your local police department, Sheriff's office, or your local office of AARP, and ask about TRIAD.

What is a TRIAD?

A TRIAD consists of a three-way effort among a sheriff, the police chief(s) in the county, and AARP or older/retired leadership in the area, who agree to work together to reduce the criminal victimization of older citizens and enhance the delivery of law enforcement services to this population. TRIAD provides the opportunity for the exchange of information between law enforcement and senior citizens. It focuses on reducing unwarranted fear of crime and improving the quality of life of seniors. A TRIAD is tailored to meet the needs of each town/city/county and is governed by a senior advisory council (S.A.L.T.).

Why is TRIAD Necessary?

Older Americans comprise the most rapidly growing segment of the population. One in every eight Americans is already aged 65 or older (32.3 million in 1992). Increased life expectancy is leading to new issues and problems for the criminal justice system as most communities experience a dramatic increase in the number of older persons. Calls for service, crimes, victims -- all are changing.

How Did TRIAD Get Started?

The American Association of Retired Persons (AARP), the International Association of Chiefs of Police (ICACP), and the National Sheriffs' Association (NSA) signed a cooperative agreement in 1988 to work together to reduce both criminal victimization and unwarranted fear of crime affecting older persons. The three national organizations agreed that police chiefs, sheriffs, older leaders, and Triad, work with seniors, working together, could devise better ways to reduce crimes against the elderly and enhance law enforcement services to older citizens. This, they believe, is true community policing, providing better service to a population, which appreciates, respects, and supports law enforcement.

Who Carries Out TRIAD Activities?

The senior advisory council, often called S.A.L.T. (seniors and Law Together) is the key component for the success of a TRIAD. In each community, the S.A.L.T. Council acts as an advocacy/advisory group and provides a forum for the exchange of information between seniors and law enforcement. Council members are selected and invited by the chief(s) of police, the sheriff, and someone representing older citizens -- an energetic, knowledgeable senior or someone from the Agency on Aging, AARP, RSVP, ministerial association, etc.

Council members can be a valuable source of input. They can assist in determining the concerns of the community's elderly persons, assess the availability of existing services and programs for the elderly, and recommend additional strategies. S.A.L.T. Council members may also take part in the crime prevention and victim assistance program of the TRIAD program, and help to identify potential volunteers to carry out TRIAD activities.

What Can TRIAD Do?

TRIAD is a way to involve law enforcement and older Americans. Areas with more serious crime problems may focus on crime prevention and victim assistance. Places where older persons are not often targets for crime may decide to concentrate on reassurance programs, training for law enforcement, and involving volunteers within the law enforcement agencies.

The S.A.L.T. advisory council (seniors and Lawmen Together) plans activities and programs that will involve and benefit both law enforcement and seniors. Some TRIADs sponsor:

- Crime prevention programs for older persons
- Information on how to avoid criminal victimization
- Expanded involvement in Neighborhood Watch
- Home security information and inspections
- Personal safety tips
- Knowledge of current frauds and scams
- Training in coping with telephone solicitations and door-to-door salesman
- Elder abuse prevention, recognition and reporting information
- Training for deputies and officers in communicating with and assisting older persons
- Reassurance programs for older citizens
- Telephone call-in programs by and for seniors
- Adopt-a-senior visits for shut-ins
- Buddy system for shut-ins
- Emergency preparedness plans by and for seniors
- Senior walks at parks or malls
- Senior safe shopping trips for groceries

- Victim assistance by and for seniors
- Courtwatch activities
- Refrigerator cards with emergency medical information
- Older persons volunteering within law enforcement agencies

TRIADs across the country are involved in some of these aspects, choosing activities which the S.A.L.T. Council agrees will be beneficial to citizens in that area. You never need to feel alone, afraid, or forgotten. If you or someone you know needs help or advice, it is only a phone call away. Thousands of people throughout America truly care about your safety and well-being. Call today. If not for yourself, do it to help someone else. That is what proactive crime prevention is all about.

You cannot live in this world without some risk, but don't become an alarmist and barricade yourself in your home (you're locking up the wrong person). We truly live in a world of wonder and joy, and you needn't deprive yourself of all life has to offer for senior citizens. By employing some of the crime prevention techniques you have learned in "Hard Target," and other crime prevention publications and community programs, you can greatly reduce your chances of becoming a victim. Although we can't change criminal thinking or behavior, you can take some comfort in the knowledge that thousands of decent Americans are dedicating their lives to keep you from harm's way. Crime prevention education can help keep you safe…learn all you can about becoming a hard target. Wear your new knowledge like body armor to make your environment a place of safety.

CHAPTER NINE

Child Crime Prevention

"Learning is not compulsory... neither is survival."

- W. Edwards Deming

When Do I Begin Teaching My Child About Personal Safety?
Parents often wonder at what age they can begin teaching their children about personal safety. While it would be convenient if there were a determined age, "one size" does not fit everybody. A child's ability to comprehend and practice safety skills is determined by the child's age and educational and developmental levels. It is also important that parents realize children need to model, rehearse, and practice new skills to incorporate them into their daily lives. A parent may think that by telling their child about personal safety, the child will assimilate that information into a practice of the skills.

"I've never known of a child who, when you tell them something one time, you never have to repeat it," stated Nancy A. McBride, the National Center for Missing & Exploited Children's® (NCMEC) Director of Prevention Education. "Children need repetition and reinforcement to acquire new skills, and parents are in a great position to work with their children in a calm, non-threatening manner."

Another important element for skill acquisition is reassurance. In today's world children are very aware of dangers and tragedies. Because that awareness already exists, it is self-defeating to use fear as a teaching tool, as fear tends to paralyze, not empower. Children who are taught safety concepts are better prepared to handle and protect themselves if self-confidence is what they are being taught. Communications and active listening are other vital components to success. If parents approach personal child safety in an open manner, children will be more likely to come to them with problems or concerns in their lives.

The National Center for Missing & Exploited Children has a signature safety publication, *Knowing My 8 Rules for Safety,* which is a good place for parents to begin teaching personal safety skills. The rules are simple, concise and provide encouragement and options for children who need an adult's help.

- I always check first with my parents or the person in charge before I go anywhere or get into a car, even with someone I know.
- I always check first with my parents or a trusted adult before I accept anything from anyone, even from someone I know.
- I always take a friend with me when I go places or play outside.
- I know my name, address, telephone number, and my parents' name.
- I say no if someone tries to touch me or treat me in a way that makes scared, uncomfortable, or confused.
- I know that I can tell my parents or a trusted adult if I feel scared, uncomfortable, or confused.
- It's okay to say no, and I know that there will always be someone who can help me.
- I am strong, smart, and have a right to be safe.

Lastly, parental and adult supervision is tantamount to a child's protection and safety. Children cannot be criticized or blamed for making the wrong safety choices if they are not old enough or skilled enough to make those choices.

"The responsibility for a young child's safety rests squarely on the trusted adults in that child's life," states McBride. "Parents need to do their due diligence and check out adults that have access to their children, and children are never too old for a parent or trusted adult supervision."

The more involvement a parent takes in his or her child's life, the less likely it is that the child will seek that attention from less savory and possibly dangerous sources. There are no quick fixes or gimmicks that take the place of adult supervision and concern. It's up to all of us to ensure our children's safety and protection.

National Center for Missing & Exploited Children
The Front Line Spring, 2002, Volume XXXXVI

Relatives take most of the more than 350,000 children abducted in America each year. Random abductions, while rare, are a terrifying reality of great concern to everyone. Here are some additional tips to safeguard young children.

- Teach your children in whose car they may ride. Children should be cautioned never to approach any vehicle, occupied or not, unless accompanied by a parent or trusted adult. If a stranger asks for directions or assistance, the child should tell them to ask an adult...then quickly leave.
- Create an atmosphere in your own home where your children feel safe confiding information about uncomfortable experiences. Ensure a sense of confidence in your children that you will believe them and be responsive to them if they need your immediate help, or counsel.
- Tell your children not to go out alone. Always take a friend, sister or brother.
- Discuss with your children whose homes in the neighborhood they can visit, and the boundaries in the neighborhood where there are permitted and not permitted to go.
- Don't just drop your children at malls, movies, video arcades or parks. Make sure they have supervision.

❑ If home alone, make sure they do not reveal that to callers at the door, or telephone.

My attitude about crime and violence directed at children is shaped by research and training. In "Hard Target" I've attempted to explore some of the complex trends and statistics, and offer some options for safety. However, the scope and magnitude of this problem should inspire all of us to rededicate ourselves to the safety and well being of children...any children!

Teach your children to react to an *action*...not the person. Most kids think the bad guys all *look* like bad guys. Teach your children to avoid confrontation and contact, and stress the point that physical appearance has nothing to do with intention.

Most importantly, let your children know they have your permission to react. Scream, yell, or run if their intuition tells them something is wrong. Kids need to know you will support their actions without fear of ridicule or admonishment. Unfortunately, children have an innate sense of trust when around strangers, especially friendly strangers, but you can teach them how to interact in a way that provides the safety they deserve. But they have to be taught. Personal child safety begins at home. Kids are like little sponges. They learn quickly. That small amount of parental training spent during their formative years is the best protective shield you can provide. Without this early training, they can easily find themselves in harm's way, and you, the parent, must then share some of the responsibility for whatever crime is perpetrated against them. That, my friend, is a heavy burden to carry.

Often emphasis is placed on the very young, but statistics tell a different story. Kids between the ages of 12 and 19, and in particular, girls, are the most victimized gender groups in the United States. In 2002, a flood of high profile child abduction, assault, and rape cases caught everyone's attention, as to the vulnerability of our older children. As tragic as these cases are, some good can be drawn from these tragedies if it motivates parents to talk to their teenagers about even rudimentary safety issues.

A universal problem with pre-teen and teenagers is the difficulty of communication. Do not let that stop you. It is natural for young people to adopt a proprietary attitude about their friends and relationships away from home. Stay the course. Calmly and quietly explain that you love them, and because of that love, your questions are about concern for their well being, and not to invade their private space. You need to know about their friends and favorite hangouts. You need to meet their friends, and the parents of their friends. You need to be involved in the lives of your children.

This excerpt from, The Front Line, Summer Issue 2002, Volume XXXXVII, National Center for Missing & Exploited Children, describes seven basic tips that should be practiced by every parent.

- Make sure that you know where each of your children is at all times. Know your children's friends and be clear with your children about the places and homes they may visit. Make it a rule that your children check in with you when they arrive at or depart from a particular location and when there is a change of plans. You should also let them know when you are running late or if your plans have changed so they can see the rule is for safety purposes and not being used to "check up" on them.
- Be involved in your children's activities. As an active participant, you'll have a better opportunity to observe how the adults in charge interact with your children. If you are concerned with someone's behavior, take it up with the sponsoring organization.
- Listen to your children. Pay attention if they tell you they don't want to be with someone or go somewhere. This may be an indication of more than a personality conflict or lack of interest in the activity or event.
- Notice when someone shows one or all of your children a great deal of attention or begins giving him or her gifts. *Take the*

time to talk to your children about the person and find out why the person is acting that way.
- Teach your children that they have a right to say "no" to any unwelcome, uncomfortable, or confusing touch or actions by others. Teach them to tell you immediately if this happens. Reassure them that you are there to help and they can tell you anything.
- Be sensitive to any changes in your children's behavior or attitude. Encourage open communication and learn how to be an active listener. Look and listen to small cues and clues that something may be troubling your children, because children are not always comfortable disclosing disturbing events or feelings. This may be because they are concerned about your reaction to their problems. If your children do confide problems to you, strive to remain calm, non-critical, and nonjudgmental. Listen compassionately to their concerns and work with them to get the help they need to resolve the problem.

Through June, NCMEC has assisted in the recovery of more than 67,000 missing children and received information on more than 80,000 cases of sexually exploited children.

NCMEC, 24-hour Toll-free Hotline: 1-800-THE-LOST
1-800-843-5678

NCMEC's Communications Center receives toll-free calls from Canada, Europe, Mexico, and the United States handles lead/sighting information received from the public; provides assistance to professionals and families in the search for missing children and attempts to assist sexually exploited children; provides safety information to help prevent the abduction and sexual exploitation of children. The NCMEC Hotline also manages the Child Pornography Tip-line on behalf of the U.S. Customs Service, U.S. Postal Inspection Service, and FBI.

ALL IT TAKES FOR EVIL TO PROSPER IS FOR GOOD MEN TO DO NOTHING!

CHAPTER TEN

Firearms

The right to protect your family and yourself is inherently fundamental. How you respond to a given situation carries with it a heavy weight of responsibility. You, as the protector, are responsible for your actions, but you do have options. You can close your eyes and hope the danger will somehow go away, without harm to you or your family, or you can react with whatever force is appropriate to the situation. Herein lies the problem. If you do nothing, chances are you will become a victim. Some victims survive, and some do not. If, on the other hand, you decide non-lethal, or lethal force is your option, you are bound by rule of law and your response must be justified, yet your adversary has no such constraints. The solution…prior crime prevention training. In every important decision in life, the most successful outcomes are a direct result of good information.

Think about it. No NFL team would even think of going on the playing field without a plan of action. No corporate executive would risk capital expenditures or expansion without a plan. No chef could prepare a banquet without a menu plan. Teachers couldn't teach, airline pilots couldn't fly, tailors couldn't design garments, builders couldn't build, and the NBA would be in shambles, with or without Magic Johnson. We even plan our funerals. The single most important ingredient in life is planning. Why wouldn't everyone want to "pre-plan" not to be a victim of crime and violence?

Chapter Ten — Firearms

Crime is multi-facetted, and your response will be determined by the threat level encountered. Simple awareness and avoidance planning will dramatically reduce your risk, and for most, that is all you will ever need to maintain your comfort level. Others will feel they need a weapon - lethal force. They are adamant in the belief that they have a right to obtain firearms for security, and the use of firearms in the defense of self, family, home, and business protection.

These "Pro-Rights" gun advocates are usually well aware of their vulnerability. With only about 150,000 police officers on active street duty in America at any given time, and with the nation's population nearing 300,000,000 inhabitants (good and evil alike), it all boils down to a number's game. Many of those same firearm advocates are also aware that it is the primary function of the police to "respond to crimes in progress, or investigate crimes committed," and not crime prevention. There are simply not enough police to protect every individual. When you call for a cop, it is usually after a crime has happened. Most citizens are at the mercy of their best decisions when confronted with a crime situation. Dialing 911 on a cell phone is not the most appropriate response to "give me your wallet or I will kill you." Therefore, if we know that a police officer is not on every corner, it is up to the citizen, him or herself, to avoid and survive criminal encounters. If you make poor choices or have no plan, you will most likely be a contributor to the problem and find yourself to be just another crime statistic.

In other words, use your God-given resources, your brain. By nature, it has been pre-programmed for survival and issued specifically to you. No permit is necessary in any state in America, or any place else in the world, and it is a state of conditioned readiness twenty-four hours a day.

Let's take a moment to discuss firearms as a deterrent and personal protection option. I am an advocate of guns for personal protection, but I do not think a firearm is appropriate for everyone, and I am not on a mission to convert those that are anti-gun. We will only explore a few pro and con issues and leave the choice in your hands.

That said, let's talk about responsible gun ownership, or non-ownership, whichever seems most appropriate for you. However, let's build our decisions on a foundation of good information, both pro and con.

Gun ownership should not carry the label "Pro-Gun." Perhaps pro-safety, or pro-responsibility would be more accurate. No one that lacks sufficient maturity and life experiences to assess various situations and make mature decisions should be allowed to own a firearm of any kind.

The technological explosion of firearm safety designs holds some of the answers. Very soon it will be common for firearms to have fingerprint recognition chip technology that will only allow the authorized registered owner to fire the weapon. No more accidental shootings by children. No more market for stolen guns. No more incidences where a police officer is killed with his own weapon. But this is only an infant step in the right direction. Who protects society from the legal gun owners that go off the deep end, and resolve conflicts with deadly force, or simply use their weapon in the commission of any crime? We also have to ask ourselves, is technology the magic cure-all? Some of the most sophisticated computer systems in the world are routinely "circumvented" by teenage children. Are we to think fingerprint recognition, or any other high-tech innovation can't be "hacked?" I am greatly encouraged by scientific breakthroughs in weapon design and safety technology, but for now, let's stick with the basic programs that teach safety and responsibility, and support tougher laws that keep firearms out of the hands of criminals.

Firearms are dangerous. They are dangerous by design. They would not be any good if they were not dangerous. Anything that makes them less dangerous can actually increase your risk. Smaller caliber, less velocity, rubber bullets, and even trigger locks are not the answer. Training and responsibility are the answer.

Mafia informant, Sammy "The Bull" Gravano, when asked about gun control said, "Gun control is the best thing you can do for crooks and gangsters. Speaking for the bad guys, I don't want you to have any defense. If I'm a bad guy, and I'm always gonna have a gun. Safety locks? You pull the trigger with a lock on it, and I'll pull the trigger on my gun...we'll see who wins."

Pro-gun, and anti-gun alike, when the heat of debate cools down and both sides fall silent in unresolved frustration, both will heartily agree on one point...for personal safety, firearms are the option of last resort.

FOOD FOR THOUGHT: *If suddenly confronted by crime and violence, the choices most citizens make, with no crime management training, are not very comforting considering they are the only non-professional present.*

The National Rifle Association (NRA), does not encourage firearm ownership. They do support your constitutional right to own a firearm, and they are strong advocates of a responsible and well trained owner. Many people buy a firearm as a protective device, keep it hidden for that day when it might be needed, yet have very little, or no working knowledge of weapons of deadly force. Those same gun owners have not taken the time and effort to familiarize themselves with the laws pertaining to deadly force, and are most often not psychologically equipped to handle the decision process that is required to use that force, much less deal with the aftermath. That takes training, both physical and mental. There is nothing wrong with someone wanting to protect themselves and their property. How you do that must conform to the law, and the dictates of common sense and good judgment - all of which are learned behavior patterns.

Where to begin? I might suggest the NRA Basic Pistol Course Program. After you have mastered that training, basic skills of safe gun handling, shooting, firearm safety and weapon maintenance, you can move to the next level — Basic Personal Protection in the Home Course. This is an adult program defined by applicable federal, state, or local law. Considerably more than "basic training," this course will focus on the safe and efficient use of a handgun for protection of self and family, and provide information on your rights to self-defense. For additional information on all of the available activities for yourself and family, you are encouraged

Chapter Ten — Firearms

to contact your local chapter of the NRA, or the national headquarters. If you are going to use a firearm for self-defense, this is the best place to begin.

Self-defense, by law, is the defense of one's person or property from threatened violence or injury by the exercise of force. In most jurisdictions of the United States, a person may practice self-defense against unlawful attack, provided the person uses no more force than is necessary to accomplish that result. Forcible resistance may not be carried to the point of taking life when it is otherwise possible to retreat. The law of defense of property is the same as that relating to the defense of the person, except that under no circumstance is the taking of life as a means of protecting property justifiable.

— **Encarta Encyclopedia Article Titled "Self Defense"**

Here are a few arguments, pro and con. The fine choice is yours. Before you make that final decision, I hope you do your homework. Go to your public library, or research the Internet. After a thorough examination of the issues, you should be more comfortable in that decision. I would also suggest you involve your family; after all, that is the underling reason for owning or not owning a firearm.

PRO: Never yield ground. It is cheaper to hold what you have than to retake what you have lost. — *General George S. Patton, Jr.*

CON: Having a firearm in the home is more dangerous than protective. — *Consumer Federation of America.*

PRO: A privately owned gun saves a life every 1.3 minutes. — *Gary Fleck and Marc Gertz, Journal of Criminal Law & Criminology, Northwestern University School of Law.*

CON: Every day, firearms kill 12 children. — *National Center for Health Statistics.*

PRO: U.S. Attorney General John Ashcroft and the Bush Administration have clearly stated their view that the Second Amendment guarantees an individual the right to keep and bear arms.

Chapter Ten — Firearms

CON: Gun related deaths are the second leading cause of injury and death in the United States. — *1998 National Vital Statistic Report.*

PRO: There were at least 400,000 fewer crimes due to civilian self-defense use of guns, and civilians deter at least 800,000 violent crimes because of gun ownership and use. — Lawrence Southwick, Jr., *"Guns and Justifiable Homicide: Deterrent and Defense."*

CON: Having one or more guns in the home makes a woman 7.2 times more likely to be a victim of domestic homicide. *Bailey (1997) Risk factors for violent death of women in the home, Archives of Internal Medicine.*

PRO: In 83.5% of successful civilian firearm self defenses, the attacker either threatened or used force first — disproving the myth that having guns available for defense wouldn't make any difference. — *Florida State University, Self-Defense Study.*

The decision to own or not to own firearms is an important choice that can only be made by you and your immediate family. Taking a pro–gun position, or electing to reject firearms as a protective barrier to crime and violence should be made only after careful consideration of all the facts. Bookstores, libraries, and the Internet will provide hundreds of information sources to help with your decision. Study the issues. Weigh the pros and cons and then use your best judgment. Keep in mind that aside from sport shooting, a handgun has one primary function, to kill another human. Once you have done all in your power to detect and evade a potentially deadly confrontation, you must be well trained and unhesitating in your decision to use deadly force. Your life will depend on it.

CHAPTER ELEVEN
Non-Lethal Self Defense

In the previous chapter, we discussed, in limited detail, firearms as a means of self-defense. I stand firm in my conviction that firearms should be the option of last resort. While fully aware that a firearm offers a powerful psychological deterrent factor, and provides the physical force necessary to stop life threatening aggression, it is not always the best response. You do not have the legal right to use deadly force unless you are confronted by deadly force. If you use this force, and fail to comply with the law, you could find yourself in prison, or mired down in lengthy and costly litigation. Of course, there are gray areas to this rule of thought, and jurisdictional boundaries differ on the actual laws as they apply to use of deadly force. That in mind, unless you are well versed in the firearm deadly force laws in your state, well trained in the use of firearms, and are mentally prepared to take another life and live with the consequences, you should consider firearm ownership very carefully.

The most sensible crime prevention safeguards are awareness, avoidance evasion, and escape. Be aware of your environment and avoiding a potential confrontation. Can everyone always know when he or she is brushing elbows with danger? Of course not. For that reason, let us discuss some non-lethal options that can offer a high degree of protection if you suddenly find yourself face-to-face with physical danger.

SELF-DEFENSE PHYSICAL TRAINING

Over the last twenty years, martial arts schools have taken the country by storm. Adults and children alike have been signing up to receive martial arts training, in one form or another, believing that physical and self defense training will protect them from some future confrontation with a bad guy. I have no problem with most of these schools.

However, it should be clearly understood that most martial arts requires years of training to be effective against personal assaults. Secondly, those acquired skills do little for those students that are unprepared psychologically and emotionally to defend themselves against a determined aggressor.

I do like the physical and mental training aspect of martial arts, and the self-discipline associated with training. In addition, a fast-paced contact sport can be enjoyable for the entire family. However, all too often, people take these courses for all the wrong reasons, and for most schools (Dojo's) there is virtually no student screening that determines the emotional reasons for this specialized training.

Can the average student of martial arts, with limited training, demonstrate his newfound skills effectively if someone suddenly steps out of a dark alley and says, "Give me your money or I will cut your throat with this straight razor?" I will let you be the best judge of that scenario.

If martial arts appeal to you, by all means, study the disciplines, have fun, win some trophies, but do not overload yourself with the belief that it is the magic panacea for personal and violent confrontation.

PERSONAL ALARMS

Putting the "Bruce Lee" approach aside for the moment, a personal protection option gaining in popularity is the "Portable Audible Alarm." These sounding devices are usually about the size of a pager, easily attach to your belt, or purse, and when activated omit a piercing 100 to 130 decibel sound designed to draw attention to someone in a crisis mode (under attack or threat of robbery), and scare off the perpetrator.

The following are some variations of these warning devices.

- **Key-Chain Alarms w/strobe light** combines two deterrents against attack... a 125db alarm and a high density flashing strobe light. Usually the size of a small cell phone, and completely legal if used properly (not for playing pranks in a crowded theatre. That would be illegal).
- **Door Stopper Alarms** that activates a shrill high dB miniature siren when a forced or unauthorized entry is attempted through a closed door.
- **2 in 1 Alarm** is a dual-purpose portable alarm that acts as a burglar alarm and a personal panic alarm. Hung on a doorknob, it instantly and automatically activates a high decibel sound when an intruder touches the doorknob. Carried on your person, it can be activated by simply pulling a pin connected to the hand strap.
- **Luggage Alarm.** This battery-powered device consists of a very small radio frequency sending unit and 120-decibel sounder, which attaches to your luggage, and a belt clipped receiver. If someone takes your luggage, laptop, or briefcase by stealth, the alarm will activate when the stolen item gets over 25 feet from the receiver. (Very nerve-racking to a thief to be walking with stolen property that suddenly starts screeching).
- **Child-Safe Alarm.** A belt-clipped high decibel alarm with push button activation. Not bad devices to ward off child

Chapter Eleven   Non-Lethal Self Defense

molesters, but most children are not responsible enough to keep from playing with a device of this nature. This could be very disruptive in a classroom environment. Also, the little boy that cried wolf comes to mind.

The list is endless. Sonic alarms, portable security strobes, and an infinite variety of whistles to blow in the face of danger. Personal alarms help, but remember, they will only deter some of the assailants some of the time, not all the assailants all of the time. I like devices like these because most perpetrators like to commit their crimes under cover of darkness, by stealth, or certainly without attracting attention. Loud sounds such as a scream, whistle, or alarm are effective in causing the thief or attacker to abandon that target and move on to greener pastures. It won't have any rehabilitative effect, and they will still lead a life of crime and violence, but it could very well identify you as an undesirably hard target.

COUNTERMEASURE PRODUCTS

- **KUBOTANS** are key-chain weapons that are easily accessible for self-defense purposes. This weapon requires martial arts training, and if used to its maximum potential, can be lethal. These devices usually have age restrictions, and may not be legal in all states.
- **COLLAPSIBLE STEEL BATONS** are primarily used by law enforcement officers, and are a replacement for outdated wooden nightsticks, A metal sleeved hand held shell with one or two solid steel shafts that extend with a simple snap of the wrist, and lock in that extended positions of 12, 16, 18, or 24 inch. Legal in many states, and can be lethal. They require training to use effectively, but in some states are sold over the counter to anyone over the age of 18. Easy to conceal, and could, under the right circumstances, be termed deadly force weapons.

Chapter Eleven — Non-Lethal Self Defense

- **NUM-CHUCKS** are martial arts weapons consisting of two wooden or metal handles connected by a length of chain. Extremely effective as a defensive or offensive weapon. Num-Chucks require martial arts training, but can be self-taught. May or may not be legal in your area, and age use restrictions might apply. Num-Chucks can be considered deadly force under the right circumstances.
- **PENKNIVES** are ballpoint pens that quickly pull apart to reveal a sharp pointed stiletto. Considered a concealed weapon in most jurisdictions, yet widely available and sold under the guise of being a letter opener.
- **BRASS KNUCKLES** are vicious, offensive and defensive weapons, and often sold by retail stores as a novelty "paper weight." Legal to sell as a novelty but illegal to use illegally (go figure).

These are only a fraction of the personal injury weapons available across America. Because they are a reality, and someone armed with them may someday approach you, <u>now</u> is the time to develop a personal safety strategy that will keep you from harm's way - not when you hear the rattle of chains, or the flash of a knife blade on a deserted street corner.

A total of 25.9 million violent and property victimizations occurred in the United States in 2000. **Bureau of Justice Statistics, U.S. Department of Justice**

STUN GUNS are another defensive self-protection option that has good points and bad points. Let's use one popular brand name stun gun as an example. The **Stun-Master** hand held stun gun delivers from 100,000 to 300,000 volts of stopping power. Powered with 9-volt batteries, these snappy devices deliver high voltage, low amperage shock, causing rapid loss of balance and muscle control, confusion, and disorientation when pressed against an aggressor. The manufacturer claims no permanent damage, and when activated a short distance from an attacker, omits a loud crackling noise accompanied by an angry, and very visible, electrical sparking across two contact points. For many assailants, this is all they need to see, much less feel. Most will get the message and back off, thus allowing you to get in the wind (run baby, run).

On the down side, I have actually witnessed someone taking a full and sustained charge from a stun gun, and smile. Size, body weight, mental state, and drugs can often render these charges almost harmless, and allow them to continue their attack. The second down side, and possibly the most important, the defender has to make body contact with the assailant—sometimes for five or ten seconds. That is awfully close and personal, and those seconds seem like hours when wired to a raging street thug.

Stun guns (Also available as stun batons) have some value as an escape and evasion tool, but they obviously have drawbacks. For instance, a dead battery comes to mind.

Air Tasers takes stun technology to its highest protection level, and is said to offer almost 100% effectiveness in stopping an assailant, in seconds, from up to 15 feet away, and has a higher instant incapacitation rate than a 9mm handgun, and when used properly, the manufacturer claims this device is non-lethal.

Air Tasers are available as a simple hand-held device. The more sophisticated advanced M18-L pistol style (There may even be a newer model on the market since my research), is equipped with an integrated laser sight, but they all work on the same technology principal.

A typical Air Taser Kit consists of the power handle (Taser), two air cartridges, owner's manual, thirty-minute training video, 9-volt battery, and a lifetime warranty. This technologically advanced weapon uses compressed air to fire two small barbed probes secured to 15 feet of Taser wire. When the probes attach to an assailant's clothing, the Air Taser sends powerful T-Waves through the wires into the body of the assailant, effectively jamming the nervous system and causing incapacitation for several minutes. No long-term damage occurs, and the Air Taser can be used as a contact stun gun.

Expensive but effective, the Air Taser is widely used by law enforcement and government agencies for use where deadly force is inappropriate, and the hazards of close physical contact need to be minimized, while effectiveness is maximized. Legal in most states, but age requirements might apply.

TASER® INTERNATIONAL 7860 E. McClain Drive, Suite #2, Scottsdale, AZ. 85260 Website: http://www.taser.com

PEPPER SPRAY

Pepper spray, commonly referred to as OC Spray, is authorized for use by most law enforcement agencies in the United States as a use-of-force option to subdue and control dangerous, combative, and violent subjects. It is recognized effective as a non-lethal personal defense option, and a personal restraint tool. It is widely available to the public in most states.

What is OC spray? The OC stands for oleoresin capsicum, which is the oily extract of the cayenne pepper plant. Exposure to OC irritates the skin, eyes, and mucous membranes of the upper respiratory tract. These properties of the pepper plant have been known for centuries. In Japan, samurai warriors threw rice paper bags filled with pepper extracts at the eyes of their enemies to cause temporary blindness. Chinese soldiers heated red peppers in hot oil to form an irritant smoke to be blown over enemy lines.

I know, that's ancient history, but every good product has to have a beginning, and that is just a thumbnail picture of how pepper spray was born.

The first trial use was by the FBI and the U.S. Mail Service in 1973, to harmlessly incapacitate humans and animals. By the late

1980's, it was broadly accepted by law enforcement agencies nationwide. With the compelling success of this unique product to fend off aggressive assailants and animals alike, it was soon in great demand by law-abiding citizens that wanted protection without the consequences of deadly force. Pepper spray was the violence restraint tool that quickly took many citizens from passive, and afraid, to defiant and proactive. Everyone had been waiting for this equalizer. Now an honest person could *refuse* to be a victim, and survive many violent encounters.

❖ One violent crime takes place every **5 seconds** in America.
   Bureau of Justice Statistics (2001), Criminal Victimization Changes.

I am a **big** advocate of pepper spray for one very good reason; there are three primary elements that allow someone to commit a criminal act.

1. Desire
2. Ability
3. Opportunity

Think of these elements as a triangle. Desire at an angle on one side, ability on the other side, and opportunity across the bottom. As with any triangle, if a single leg is missing, a triangle cannot be formed. This is also true with a crime triangle. Take any one of these elements away, desire, ability, or opportunity, and a crime is highly unlikely to occur.

A well-placed shot of pepper spray can quickly wash away *desire*, weaken *ability* to the point of incapacity, and certainly make any perceived *opportunity* a risky, and undesirable venture.

Let us take a few minutes to examine the benefits of pepper spray in relation to your personal safety strategy. As you lay the groundwork for your safety plan, think of pepper spray as one of the cornerstones to support a solid crime prevention foundation. Here is why!

To this point, Hard Target has been about methods and ideas to assist you in understanding the problems associated with crime and violence. And evaluating, planning, implementing, and improving on your security. This book would not be complete without leaving you with a solid understanding of the defensive values of pepper spray. What you do with this information is your decision. I can only provide information.

OC – OLEORESIN CAPSICUM
PERSONAL DEFENSE PEPPER SPRAYS

Oleoresin Capsicum (OC), commonly referred to as "Pepper Spray, is the preferred tactical product to incapacitate violent or threatening subjects. First documented as effective by law enforcement and military, it is now legally available in most states for private citizen personal protection.

Like any other personal protection products, there are benefits and limitations.

Benefits of Pepper Spray

- The physical effects of OC significantly reduce aggressive behavior.
- Effective for aggressors under the influence of drugs, alcohol, or mental impairment.
- No apparent long-term effects.
- Few medical side effects.
- Considered a non-lethal response protocol.
- Limited training needed.
- Effective against many wild animals.
- Variety of unit sizes and spray patterns.
- Effective aggressor defense without close contact.
- Effective with multiple assailants.

Limitations of Pepper Spray

- Avoid use around flame.

- May contain other chemicals that pose health or safety hazards.

- Suspect must be within effective range.

- Unstable in high wind, and close confinement activation.

- Effectiveness reduced by eyewear, masks, or hands used as defensive barrier.

- Inadequate training or improper use can reduce incapacitation time.

- If proper control and use is not maintained, OC spray canister can be taken from the defender and used by the assailant.

- High vehicle temperature can cause aerosol can to leak, rupture, or explode.

- Respiratory inflammation possible with user pre-diagnosed with respiratory problems.

- May be illegal in some jurisdictions.

- No chemical agent is 100% effective, 100% of the time.

Back in 1912, a pharmacologist named Wilber Scoville set the test standards for heat rating of pepper spray - called the Scoville Organoleptic Test. Today the heating value of OC is established through modern technology, a computerized method called high performance liquid chromatography. The pepper heat scales range from zero Scoville units for bell pepper, to over 5,000 for a Jalapeno, and a very hot 2,000,000 to 300,000 for a Habanera (said to be the hottest pepper in the world). Pure capsaicum oil extract is 15,000.

Most sprays contain 10% to 15% OC formula, and a 1.5 to 2 million Scoville heat rating. Aside from hot, many defensive sprays contain an ultraviolet identifying dye for easy identity and apprehension of the attacker. Many manufacturers will replace your used container if you can establish it was used in a self-defense situation. For many reasons, our less than perfect criminal justice system for one, non-lethal weapons and the use of "less than force" is increasingly attracting the attention of citizens that are sick and tired of being a target of crime and violence. Clearly, the ability to repel and escape a criminal encounter without fear of prosecution or civil litigation is preferable over the high liability, and consequences, of deadly force response. If you cannot detect and avoid a dangerous situation, and if opportunity permits non-lethal response, it can, and has, saved many lives. For these reasons, I recommend OC pepper spray for use where legally authorized. My wife carries pepper spray, my daughter carries pepper spray, I carry pepper spray, and thousands of police officers carry pepper spray. Why wouldn't you want that same measure of protection?

This book has covered a broad spectrum of crime and violence, awareness and avoidance, and personal defense options. Many of my readers will take this information in the spirit for which it was intended, and begin building a personal safety plan before they become victims – unfortunately, others will view Hard Target as moderately interesting, mildly humorous, and close these pages and walk away with the same skepticism they had when they first read the introduction. Sadly, there is nothing I or any other crime prevention practitioner can do for that individual except offer a silent prayer, and hope someone in the near future can get his or her attention.

Crime and violence, for the foreseeable future, really *is* in the DNA of our society. Don't let apathy make you a victim. You really can refuse to be a victim.